ROYAL ICED
CHRISTMAS
CAKES

Festive cakes made easy

~

LINDSAY JOHN BRADSHAW

LINDSAY JOHN BRADSHAW

MEREHURST
LONDON

This book is dedicated to my niece, Megan

Published 1987 by Merehurst Limited
Ferry House, 51-57 Lacy Road,
Putney, London SW15 1PR

Reprinted 1988, 1990, 1991 (twice), 1992

© Copyright 1987 Merehurst Limited

ISBN 1 85391 195 X

A catalogue record for this book is available from the British Library.

Managing Editor: Joyce Becker
Editor: Suzanne Ellis
Designer: Roger Daniels
Cover Design: Peter Bridgewater
Step-by-step Photography: Lindsay John Bradshaw
Cake Photography: John Todd of Carlton Studios (Manchester) and
John Johnson of John Johnson Photography
Typeset by: Lineage, Watford
Colour Separation by: Fotographics Ltd, London-Hong Kong
Printed in Belgium by Proost International Book Production, Turnhout.

Author's Acknowledgements
I would like to thank the many sugarcraft enthusiasts who regularly
support my cake decorating demonstrations, and prompted the idea of
a Christmas cake book. Without these friends continually asking for
cake patterns, templates and advice on design ideas, this book would
not have been written. Thanks also to my family for their encouragement
and patience during the many months of photography and writing.

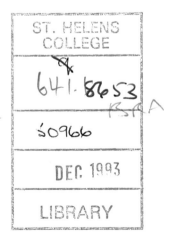

Contents

Foreword

I came into the teaching side of the bakery industry in 1959 and cake design and decoration became my first love. Every so often you discover a gem of a student; Lindsay John Bradshaw was such a student, attaining a very high standard of design and decoration.

His book contains full instructions on how to decorate Christmas cakes with royal icing, from the simplest type of design up to designs that will challenge the more competent cake decorator.

A frequent complaint I hear from cake decorators is that they cannot use a design they see in a book, and they do not know how to re-draw it to the required size. *Royal Iced Christmas Cakes* offers a whole series of designs with working templates suitable for the popular 20cm (8in) cake.

This is a wonderful design ideas book with step-by-step photographs showing how to produce the cakes. Anyone who enjoys cake decorating will appreciate the talent, craftsmanship and professionalism of the author.

R. J. Oakes L.C.G.
Senior Lecturer in charge of Cake Design and Decoration
Salford College of Technology

Introduction

Christmas is an important season in the cake decorator's year, and even people who make only one or two cakes each year want to produce a fabulous creation for Christmas. *Royal Iced Christmas Cakes* is a complete pattern book and step-by-step guide to decorating 23 original designs for holiday cakes using the traditional medium of royal icing.

Royal Iced Christmas Cakes features actual-sized patterns and templates for each cake, most based on the popular family-sized 20cm (8in) round and square cakes. Each design and motif is clearly reproduced so that the cake decorator can trace directly from the book and begin icing immediately.

The step-by-step instructions are all illustrated with colour photographs of each important stage, making the directions clear and simple to follow. There is also a large, full colour photograph of each finished cake, plus close-up actual size photographs of important details.

The author, Lindsay John Bradshaw, has several years experience in teaching cake decoration at college level. Trained as a baker and confectioner he now specializes in art and design in confectionery, and in this book he shares his great gifts in Christmas cake design. His training as a teacher means that the instructions are clear and easy to follow even for the novice decorator, and his wonderful new ideas will appeal to sugarcraft artists at all levels.

Making Leaves and Flowers

A book entirely devoted to decorating Christmas Cakes will inevitably feature numerous edible holly leaves, Christmas roses, pine branches and fir cones. To avoid repetition, the various methods for making all leaves and flowers are illustrated and described in this section of the book. The step-by-step instructions for several of the cakes in the book will refer to leaves and flowers produced using a particular method. Simply refer back to this section for full instructions.

Sugarpaste Leaves

Use sugarpaste or flower paste. Roll green paste out to the thickness required by the size of the leaf. The smaller the leaf, the thinner the paste should be. Cut out holly leaves using cutters of the required size. Do not cut out too many holly leaves at one time or the paste may crust over before you have time to mark and form them. Mark veins on the leaves using a modelling tool or the back of a small knife.

To obtain natural curves, position the leaves in pieces of crumpled foil. Curve each leaf in a different position for use in sprays or arrangements, or dry them all with the same curve for cake sides or corners where a set shape is necessary.

Another method of drying is to place the leaves over curved formers after marking. The leaves may also be dried flat. When completely dry, extra green and brown tones may be added by using a dry paintbrush and petal dust or with an aerograph spray and liquid food colouring. Edible silver or gold colouring painted on the leaves gives an elegant finish.

Piped Leaves

Use a No1 or No2 tube, depending upon the size of leaf required, to pipe the shape shown onto waxed paper, with green royal icing.
To pipe, start with a narrow point, then apply more pressure to the piping bag to form a bold centre. Taper off to a point. Before the icing begins to crust, use a fine paintbrush to pull out points as shown. Pull out one point at each end, followed by three or four points on each side. The side points should radiate from the centre of the leaf. Leave

the brush lines in the icing, emphasizing them as necessary to represent the veins.
Do not pipe out too many leaf shapes at once or the icing will crust before the detail is applied.

Allow to dry flat, or over curved formers as shown. Apply green and brown tones by using a dry paintbrush and edible petal dust, or use an aerograph.
When dry remove from waxed paper. These leaves can also be piped directly onto a royal iced surface or a sugarpaste plaque.

Tulle Leaves

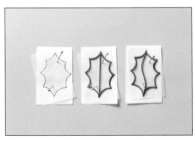

Cut holly leaves from green tulle using the template. Place the template onto a piece of thick card or cakeboard and cover with a piece of waxed paper. Pin the tulle taut over the template. Use a No1 or No2 tube, depending upon the size, and green royal icing, to pipe a line down the middle of the tulle. Pipe a straight line, or a more natural curved one. Pipe the holly leaf following the edge of the tulle. Allow the leaves to dry.

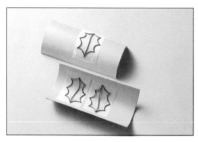

For a more attractively shaped leaf, use a curved former. Secure the waxed paper to the former with masking tape. Pin the tulle leaf over the template and waxed paper, then pipe as for flat tulle leaves. Allow to dry.

Stencilled Leaves

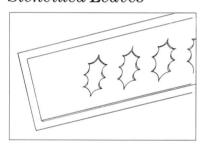

1 Make a tracing of the size of holly leaf you require, using the templates. Transfer the tracing onto thin card, or use oiled stencil paper for a more durable stencil. Trace the required number of leaves all on the same piece of card. Neatly cut out the shapes using a sharp craft knife.

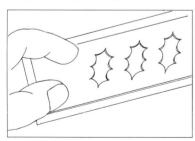

2 Place the stencil onto waxed paper, ensuring that all cut out sections are on the waxed paper. With forefinger and thumb, hold the stencil firmly on the waxed surface. Do not allow the stencil or waxed paper to move.

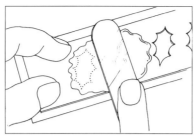

3 Use a palette knife to spread a small amount of green royal icing across the stencil to cover the required number of cut outs. Spread from the end of the stencil held by the finger and thumb to the unheld end as shown. Spreading the opposite way may cause the stencil and waxed paper to buckle and lift.

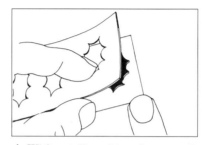

4 Without disturbing the stencil hold the waxed paper firmly on the work surface. Starting at the end of the stencil where the waxed paper is being held, gently lift the stencil, and peel off. Allow the stencils to dry flat or on curved formers.
The dry leaves may be used as they are, or coloured with tones of green and brown. The colour may be applied with a dry brush and petal dust, or use an aerograph spray.

Piped Outline Leaves

Prepare a template of a holly leaf. Place a piece of waxed paper over the template, securing with masking tape or small dots of icing at each corner. Pipe the outline and centre vein with green icing and a No1 or No2 tube, depending on the size of leaf. Allow the leaves to dry flat or over curved formers.

Runout Leaves

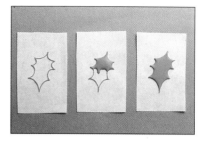

Follow the instructions for piped outline leaves, then flood in with green runout icing. The centre vein may be omitted or retained. If the vein is retained and the flooding of each side of the leaf is carried out separately, allow the first half to skin over before flooding in the other side.

Allow the leaves to dry flat or over curved formers. Apply green and brown tones using a dry paintbrush and edible petal dust, or an aerograph spray. The leaves could also be painted with food colour to give more detail.

Holly leaf templates

Modelled Christmas Roses

Use white sugarpaste or flower paste and cornflour (cornstarch) for rolling. Roll out the paste until almost translucent. Cut out petals with a Christmas rose cutter of the required size; cut five petals for each flower. If you do not have cutters, prepare a thin card template from the petal outlines. Cut round the template on the rolled out paste. Use a ball tool to cup shape each petal, then place immediately onto crumpled tin foil to create natural curves. Allow to dry completely.

Make formers from plastic or polystyrene (styrofoam) egg boxes or fruit trays; or use plasticine as described for stencilled flowers. Line each former with a small circle of waxed paper. Pipe a small bulb of white icing in the centre and arrange five petals, slightly overlapping with points facing outwards. Secure the petals to the centre bulb; let dry.
Apply a small amount of greenish-yellow colour to the centre of the flower to give its characteristic waxy appearance. Apply the colour with a dry brush and petal dust, or use an aerograph spray.
To complete the flower, pipe a small bulb of egg-yellow coloured icing in the centre and insert a few small stamens. For tiny stamens, use cut stamen wires, with the ends delicately touched in slightly softened yellow icing.

Piped Christmas Roses

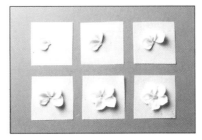

Following the sequence shown, place a small square of waxed paper onto a flower nail and pipe five petals using a No57, 58 or 59 petal tube. Put a small amount of yellow-green icing down one side of the icing bag and white icing in the remaining space. Position the yellow-green icing to come out of the wide end of the petal tube. Use stiff, well beaten icing to retain a good shape.

Allow the flowers to dry on the waxed paper, then pipe a small yellow bulb in the centre using a No1 tube. Place the flower face downwards into some yellow-coloured caster (superfine) sugar. Remove from the sugar and shake off any excess.

Stencilled Christmas Roses

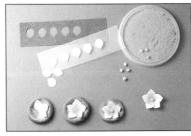

Make a tracing of the size of petal required, using the templates. Follow the instructions for stencilled leaves up to and including step 4. Allow the stencilled petal shapes to dry.

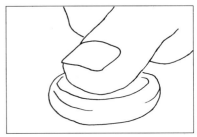

1 To make formers for assembling the flowers; mould small balls of sugarpaste, marzipan or plasticine and press onto a cake board.

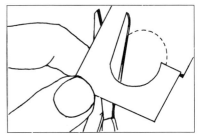

2 Cut out small circles of waxed paper.

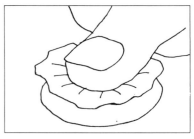

3 Place a waxed paper circle into each former and press using finger or thumb to produce an even cup shape.

4 Pipe a small dot of royal icing in centre of waxed paper. Position five petals in the former, points facing outwards. Ensure each petal is secured to the piped dot. Allow to dry.

5 Colour the centre of each flower yellow-green with edible petal dust or spray with liquid colour. Prepare flower centres by piping small bulbs of icing into yellow caster (superfine) sugar; allow to dry and attach one to each flower centre.

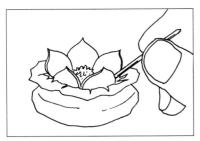

6 Leave the finished flower to dry in the formers, and then use a cocktail stick between the flower and the waxed paper to gently release the flower. Remove the cocktail stick and gently lift out the flower. Place into position on cake, attaching with a small bulb of royal icing.

Marzipan Pine Cones

Use brown marzipan to form a cone slightly smaller than the required size of the finished pine cone. Place onto a cocktail stick. Roll several small balls of marzipan; cover to prevent crusting.

Flatten each ball between thumb and finger as it is attached to the cone. Start with two petals at the top, then build downwards with overlapping rows of petals, as shown. The petals should stick without moistening, if not lightly brush the cone with egg white to attach.

Press the cocktail stick into a polystyrene block and allow the finished pine cone to firm up before use.

Piped Pine Branches

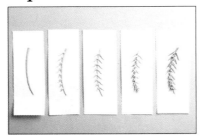

Make a tracing of the required size of pine branch, using the template provided. Place a piece of waxed paper over the drawing. Using a No 1 tube and green icing, pipe the branches following the sequence shown. Side spikes are pulled out to a point while piping. When dry brush with edible petal dust or use an aerograph spray to apply tones of brown and green.

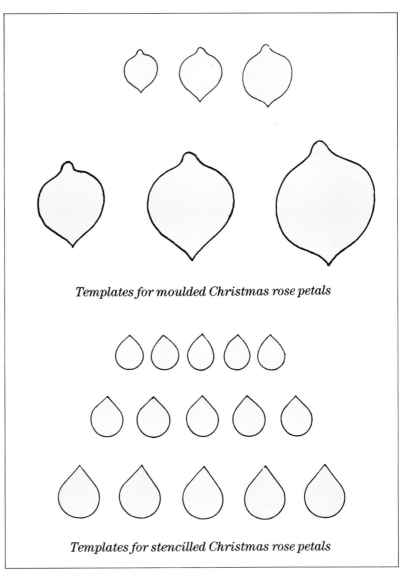

Templates for moulded Christmas rose petals

Templates for stencilled Christmas rose petals

Party Time

*A bright and attractive design
using traditional white with
Christmas red and green, yet with
a modern style of decoration.
Almost all the decoration is
prepared off the cake, even the
lettering and the unusual
side decoration.*

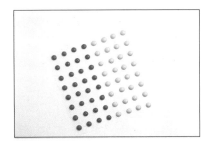

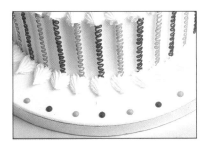

1 Coat a 20cm (8in) round cake top, sides and board with white icing. Prepare the cake side decorations. Pipe straight lines of white icing onto waxed paper using No44 tube. The lines should be the same length as the depth of the cake side. Draw two lines of the required distance onto paper, and use as guide under the waxed paper.

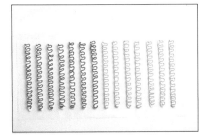

2 When the lines are completely dry, pipe a wavy line along each one using a No1 tube. Finish half of the lines with red wavy lines and half with green.

3 Prepare the runout Father Christmas, outline onto waxed paper with chocolate-coloured icing and No1 tube. Flood in separate sections with the colours as shown. Allow sections to skin over before flooding adjacent sections. Pipe the belt buckle on waxed paper, allow to dry, then paint with gold edible food colouring. Attach belt buckle to figure.

4 Pipe out some small red and green bulbs with slightly softened icing onto waxed paper.

5 Trace lettering outline onto paper. Place a piece of waxed paper over the drawing and outline with chocolate-coloured icing and a No1 tube. Flood in the letters with red, white and green runout icing.

6 Remove side lines from waxed paper and attach to the cake side as shown with a little white icing. Alternate the line colours, red and green.

7 Next, attach alternating colours of prepared red and green bulbs around the cake board edge. Pipe shells radiating out from the centre, around the top edge and base of the cake. Use No11, 12 or 13 tube with white icing.

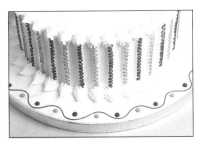

8 Pipe a wavy chocolate-coloured line with a No1 tube. Pipe the line to curve around the red and green bulbs. Paint eyes on Father Christmas and position with lettering onto cake top, attach with icing.

Father Christmas

CHRISTMAS

Reindeer

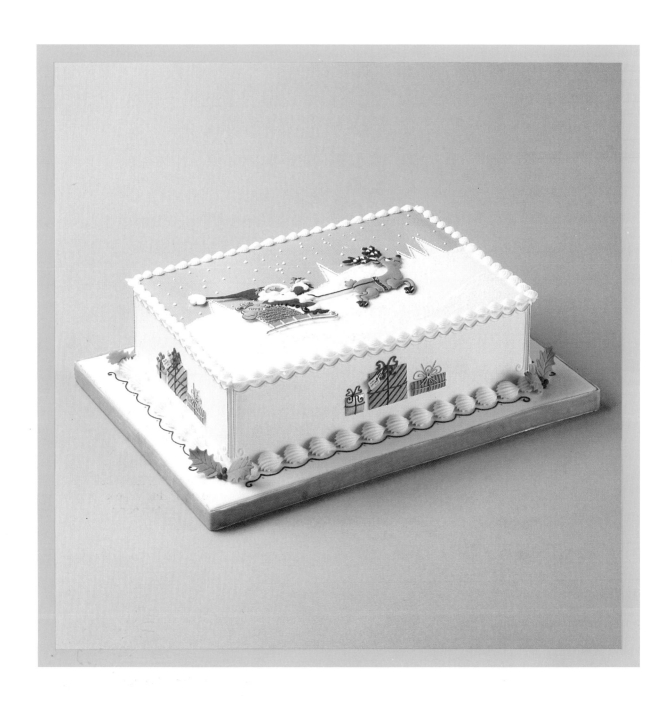

A stencil provides an easy method to make a snowscene background for Santa and his reindeer. Draw your own Christmas presents and include gift tags with names of the family.

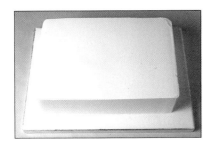

1 Coat an oblong 18 x 25cm (7 x 10in) cake top, sides and board with white icing.

2 To make the runout Santa and reindeer, trace the drawing. Place a piece of waxed paper over the tracing and outline using No1 tubes with red, white, coffee and chocolate icing. The base of the sleigh is piped using a No2 tube and white icing.

3 Flood in the separate sections with coloured runout icing. Allow sections to skin over before flooding in adjacent sections. Let dry.

4 Paint the sleigh with edible gold colouring. Pipe on the detail using a No1 tube with red and green icing. Paint the toy sack, eyes, nose, and reindeer hooves with food colouring. Pipe holly on Santa's hat, snow on the reindeer's antlers and the reindeer harness.

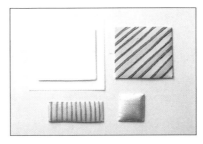

5 Using the templates, outline the parcels with white icing and a No1 tube; let dry. Paint the gift wrapping paper designs using food colouring.

6 Make a thin card template of the snowscape outline. Cut out and secure to the cake top with masking tape. Spread blue icing over the top of the cake, masking the cake sides if necessary. Flat ice as usual, pulling a straight edge over the template and across the blue icing. Remove the template and allow to dry.

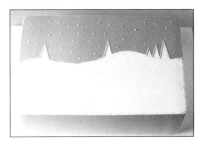

7 Pipe white icing on the tree edges using a No1 tube. With the same tube pipe several small snowballs. Brush the white piping with softened white icing and sprinkle with granulated sugar. Remove excess sugar.

8 Remove the Santa and reindeer from the waxed paper and attach to the cake top with icing. Pipe the reins with a No1 tube and white icing; overpipe with chocolate-coloured icing. Pipe a sprig of holly in Santa's hand.

Holly is piped separately

Santa on sleigh

Reins are piped directly onto cake top

Reindeer

9 Pipe shells around the top edge using a No44 tube and white icing. Pipe 2.1. linework beneath the shells and vertically down each corner. Overpipe the top line with blue icing and a No1 tube. Edge the shells with a white icing line piped using a No2 tube.

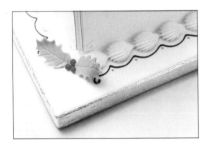

10 Pipe shells around the base using a No13 tube and white icing. Pipe a scallop next to the shell with chocolate-coloured icing and a No1 tube. Pipe a tiny blue dot on the board at each scallop join, using a No1 tube. Position two marzipan holly leaves at each corner; attach with a bulb of white icing. Pipe three red berries using a No2 tube.

11 Remove the Christmas gifts from the waxed paper and attach to cake side with white icing. Pipe the gift tie and bows onto the gifts using a No1 tube with red and white icing. Paint the white icing lines with edible gold and silver colouring. A tiny sugarpaste gift tag may also be attached. For extra detail paint on an inscription with black food colouring. To complete, attach a blue velvet ribbon to the cake board edge.

14

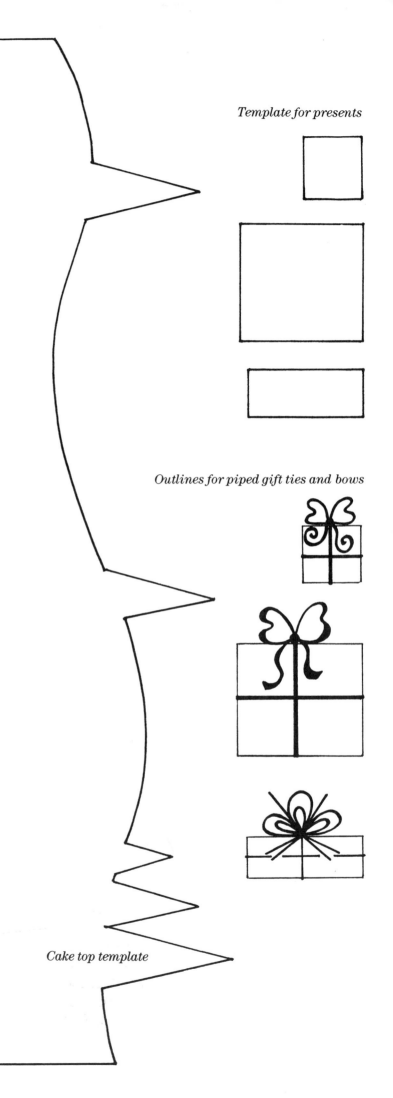

Template for presents

Outlines for piped gift ties and bows

Cake top template

Icicle

An easy design for the adventurous beginner to experiment with piping techniques and runout work. Reduce the amount, or even omit the inscription and simply position Santa's face in the centre of the cake.

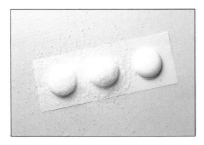

1 Coat a 20cm (8in) round cake top, sides and board with pink icing. Pipe the sugar drops for the top border using slightly softened white royal icing and a No3 tube. Soften the icing with egg white until it is between runout and bulb piping consistency. Make the drops about 1.5cm (½in) in diameter and immediately after piping, sprinkle with granulated sugar to give a frosty coating. Remove excess sugar and allow drops to dry completely.

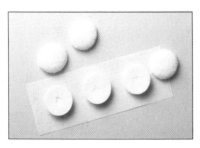

2 The granulated sugar coating will delay the drying so dry the drops as much as possible and then carefully remove from the waxed paper. Turn upsidedown to dry.

3 Make the runout Father Christmas face. Trace the outline onto drawing paper. Place a piece of waxed paper over the drawing and pipe all lines in chocolate-coloured icing using a No1 tube. Flood in each section very thinly with the coloured icing as shown. Allow sections to crust over before flooding in adjacent sections. The runout should be the same thickness as the tube used for outlining, in this case No1. Dry.

4 Paint on the eyes with black food colouring. A small holly leaf and berry may also be piped onto the hat.

5 Pipe a shell border around the base of the cake using a No32 tube and white icing. Pipe a tapering roped line on the cake board around each shell. At each join of the roped lines, pipe a holly leaf and berry, using the method described for piped leaves.

Outline for runout Father Christmas face

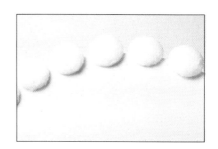

6 Attach the sugar drops to the cake top edge with small bulbs of icing. Allow to dry.

7 To finish the border, pipe icicles on each sugar drop using white icing and a No2 tube; pull down with the tube as you pipe to form a point. Attach a red ribbon and bow to the cake side.

8 Remove the face from the waxed paper and attach to the cake top with icing. Trace the lettering outline onto the cake top. Pipe the 'Hello It's' in chocolate-coloured icing using a No1 tube. Pipe 'Christmas' in red icing using a No2 tube. Attach a silver-edged, brown velvet ribbon to the cake board edge to finish.

Hello! It's Christmas

Frosty

Although this cake looks quite elaborate, very few piping skills are required, making it ideal for a beginner. Silver or coloured dragées look attractive attached to the trees.

1 Coat a 20cm (8in) round cake top with white icing. Coat sides and board with blue icing.

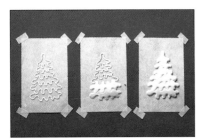

2 To make the runout Christmas trees for the side decoration, trace the design onto drawing paper. Place a piece of waxed paper over the drawing and outline in white icing using a No1 tube. Flood in with blue runout icing, working from the base upwards. Make each section paler blue by adding more white runout icing. Leave to dry. Make some small icing snowballs by piping small bulbs of white icing using a No1 tube. Sprinkle with granulated sugar, remove any excess and let dry.

3 To make the coloured background for the snowman use a dry brush and petal dust, or an aerograph spray to apply orange, violet and blue as shown.

4 Cut out a stencil of the snowman. Trace the design onto thin card or stencil paper; cut out with a sharp craft knife. Position the stencil on the cake top, securing with masking tape. Spread white icing over the cut out area, remove the stencil and sprinkle the snowman with granulated sugar. Remove excess sugar.

5 Make a paper template of the cake side panel. Measure a piece of paper 5cm (2in) wide and the same length as the cake circumference. Trace the snowscape outline onto the paper, repeating along the length. Cut out the shape. Secure the template to the upper cake side with masking tape, then stipple white icing around the base using a small piece of foam. Remove the template and immediately sprinkle with granulated sugar. Remove excess sugar.

6 Pipe icicles onto the cake board with white icing, sprinkle with granulated sugar. Remove excess sugar. Pipe a tiny plain shell around the board edge with white icing, using a No1 tube.

7 For the top edge of the cake, roll out a sausage of white marzipan about 1cm (⅜in) thick and long enough to fit around the circumference of the cake. Attach to the cake top edge with white icing, allow to set fully.

8 Use a small piece of foam to stipple the marzipan neatly with white icing. Pipe icicles around the inside edge and sprinkle with granulated sugar. Remove excess.

9 Remove the trees from the waxed paper and attach at regular intervals to the side of the cake with icing. Stick some of the prepared snowballs to the cake side around trees. Finish the snowman by piping the hat, scarf, lamp, face, broom and buttons, using No1 tubes. The scarf is piped in a zigzag, alternating two colours of icing. Brush a little white icing for the ground; sprinkle with granulated sugar. Attach a few icing snowballs. Attach a blue velvet ribbon to the cake board edge.

Hat

Snowscape panel template

Scarf

Lamp

Broom

Template for runout tree:
make eight

Snowman stencil template

19

Robin

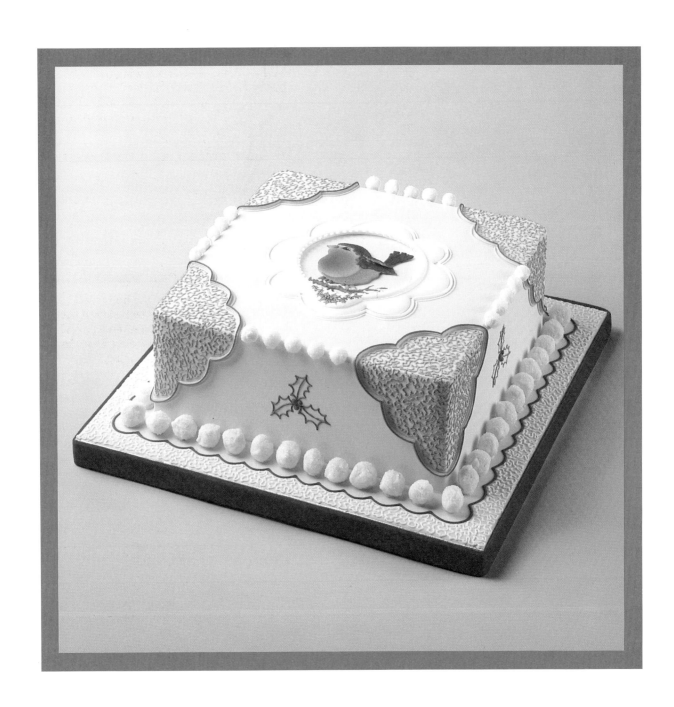

Two piping tubes only are used for the decoration on this pretty peach and green cake. The snowball border eliminates the need for piping.

1 Coat a 20cm (8in) square cake top, sides and board with pale orange icing. To make robin runout, trace robin from drawing. Place a piece of waxed paper over the drawing and outline with brown, white and coffee-coloured icing using a No1 tube. Flood in with coloured runout icing, allowing sections to skin over before flooding adjacent sections. Make runout wing. Let dry.

2 Paint robin with food colouring, brushing softened chocolate-coloured icing on body and tail to give added detail and texture. Attach wing with icing.

3 To make runout pieces for centrepiece, prepare drawings using outlines. Place waxed paper over drawings and outline with white icing using a No1 tube. Flood in with white runout icing and leave to dry.

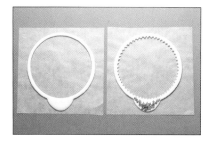

4 Paint holly leaves and berries with food colouring. Use a No1 tube with white icing to pipe a three-dot edging on the inside edge of the top ring. Let dry.

5 Stick the two runout sections together with white icing.

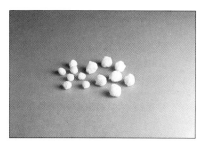

6 To make the snowballs, mould small balls of white marzipan in two sizes. Allow the balls to skin over, roll in white icing and let dry. Re-roll in icing and sprinkle with granulated sugar to give a frosty look. Allow to dry.

7 Cut a thin card template using the outline. Position the template on the cake using masking tape. Outline the shape in base colour icing using a No2 tube. Remove the template. Repeat on all side corners, and top corners as shown.

8 Using a No1 tube and green icing, pipe filigree in each of the four outlined corner sections. Following the outlines made with the No2 tube, complete 3.2.1. linework. Pipe the top line in red icing using a No2 tube.

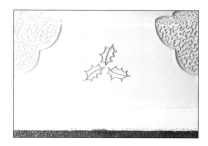

9 Transfer the holly leaf design to each side of the cake. Pipe the leaves using a No1 tube and green icing. Pipe the berries with red icing.

10 Remove the robin from the waxed paper and attach to cake top with icing. Pipe a branch beneath the robin using a No1 tube and chocolate-coloured icing. Pipe white snow and attach prepared leaves and berries.

11 Position and attach the centrepiece frame to the cake top. Pipe 3.2.1. linework around the runout edge.

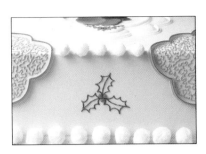

12 Attach the prepared snowballs to the cake; small ones on the top edge and larger ones around the base.

13 Pipe a scallop using a No 1 tube and chocolate-coloured icing on the board to follow the snowballs. Fill in the area between the chocolate line and the cake board edge with filigree piped using a No 1 tube and white icing. Attach a red velvet ribbon to the board.

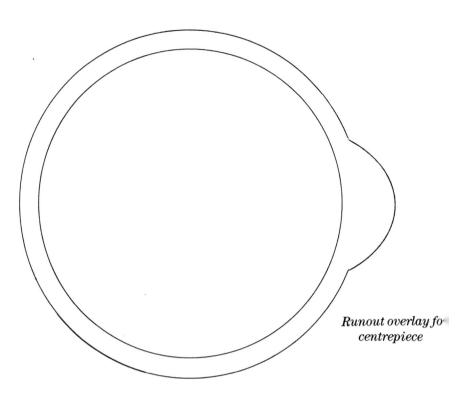

Runout overlay for centrepiece

Holly design for side panels

Robin

Corner template

Centrepiece runout

22

Ivy and Holly

*An elegant design, featuring
modelled sugarpaste ivy and holly
leaves. The sugarpaste gift tag
could be piped with a name if the
cake is a present.*

1 Coat a 20cm (8in) round cake top, sides and board with white royal icing. To prepare the ivy leaves, thinly roll out some light cream-coloured sugarpaste or flower modelling paste. Polish and smooth the surface of the paste by rubbing your palm gently over it. Cut out about 25 ivy leaves using special cutters, or make a card template from the drawing. Before the leaves start to firm up, place each one into a former of crumpled foil so they will dry in natural curves.

2 When dry, paint each leaf with food colouring. First paint light green, then add dark green blotches leaving a small margin of unpainted sugarpaste around the edge to give a variegated effect. Paint a few veins on each leaf.

3 Cut out a sugarpaste gift tag using the template or use an oval cutter. The small hole is cut out with a No3 or No4 tube. Place the tag onto a curved former as shown and allow to dry. Pipe a fine scallop around the edge of the tag using a No1 tube. Let dry. Paint the scallop with edible gold colouring. Pipe an inscription on the tag using a

IVY AND HOLLY CAKE SIDE LINEWORK TEMPLATE

1 Cut a length of drawing paper to fit around the coated cake. The paper strip should be the height of the cake side.

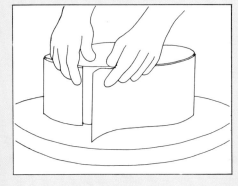

2 With the paper strip flat, draw an accurately measured line down the centre of the length of the paper.

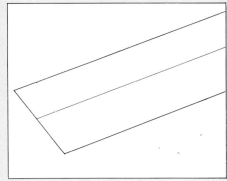

3 Measure the length of the paper and divide into 10 equal sections. Mark the measured sections on each side of the paper, then draw a line across.

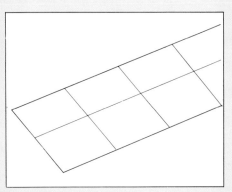

4 In each measured section draw in a suitable curve using a round object, such as a pastry cutter. Alternate the curves as shown to create a continuous wavy line.

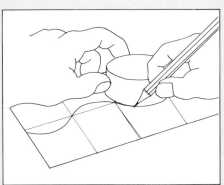

5 Cut neatly along the wavy line to produce two template shapes. Only one is needed.

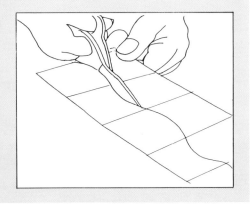

No1 tube and chocolate-coloured icing. 'Christmas Thoughts' can be traced from the drawing and piped. When dry, thread tag with gold ribbon and tie a bow.

4 Prepare a side linework template to fit the cake. Fix the template around the cake, and secure with masking tape. Tilt the cake and pipe a wavy line alongside, not touching, the template. Use a No2 tube and chocolate-coloured icing; let dry. Remove the template.

5 Pipe small, curly tendrils using a No1 tube with greenish-brown icing.

6 Attach the prepared ivy leaves with small bulbs of white icing.

7 Pipe white shells around the top edge using a No42 star tube.

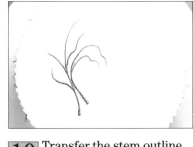

8 Pipe slightly larger white shells around the base using a No44 star tube.

9 Use a No1 tube and green icing to pipe a decorative border around the cake board edge.

10 Transfer the stem outline onto the cake top and pipe the stems using a No2 tube and chocolate-coloured icing. A few tendrils could also be piped. Arrange ivy, a few prepared sugarpaste holly leaves and piped red berries. Attach gift tag. Complete cake with green velvet ribbon attached to the cake board edge.

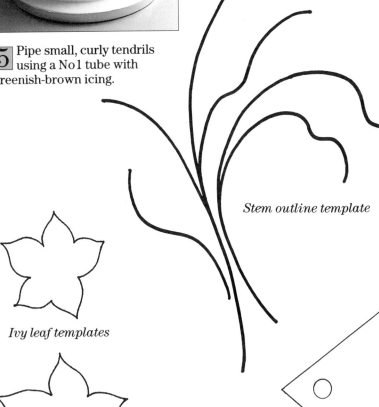

Stem outline template

Ivy leaf templates

Gift tag

Christmas Thoughts

Greetings

Grey may not be everyone's idea of
a cake colour, but with red, white
and green it makes an eyecatching
combination. The choirboys could
be replaced with a marzipan
Father Christmas or snowman.

1 Coat a 20cm (8in) round cake with grey icing. For the final side coating, use a combed scraper. Coat the board with white icing.

2 Prepare the stencilled holly leaves for the cake sides. Trace the outlines onto thin card or stencil paper. Cut out the shapes using a sharp craft knife. Place the stencil onto waxed paper. Hold the stencil and waxed paper firmly and spread green royal icing across the stencil cutout areas; remove stencil and allow leaves to dry.

3 Make three choirboys from red modelling marzipan. Roll a small cone for the body, attach a thin sausage of marzipan for the arms. Cut out a small fluted circle of white sugarpaste for the ruffle, using the template or a small flower cutter. Attach the ruffle with a little egg white. A small egg of flesh-coloured marzipan forms the head. For the mouth, insert a tiny ball of orange-red marzipan into the head using a wooden cocktail stick. Add a marzipan nose. Pipe the eyes and hair with royal icing using No1 tube.

4 Attach head to body with a little egg white. Cut a small hymn sheet from rice paper and position between arms and body.

5 Make trees by forming cones of green marzipan. Snip the cone with small scissors from the top downwards to create the branches. Allow the trees to set. Lightly brush each one with softened white royal icing, then sprinkle with granulated sugar. Make a selection of trees in various sizes.

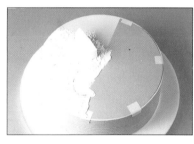

6 Using the cake top design outline cut a thin card template. Position and secure the template to the cake top with small pieces of masking tape. Use a small piece of foam sponge to stipple the exposed cake top very lightly with white icing. Sprinkle with granulated sugar and remove excess. Remove the template and let dry.

7 Transfer the inscription to the cake top. Make sure the lettering is aligned at the correct angle to the stipple work. Pipe the inscription and straight line using a No2 tube and grey icing.

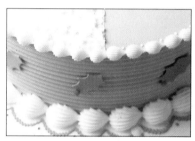

8 Overpipe with black royal icing and a No2 tube.

9 Pipe shells around top edge and base with white icing, using a No42 tube for the top and a No13 for the base. Carefully remove the stencilled holly leaves from their backing, and attach at regular intervals at an angle to the cake side. Use grey icing to attach the leaves. Pipe a neat red icing bulb on each leaf using a No2 tube to form a berry. Attach the choirboys to the cake top with small bulbs of white icing. The trees are mounted on white icing sprinkled with granulated sugar to resemble snow. Complete cake by attaching a Christmas red velvet ribbon to the cake board edge.

Greetings

Cake edge

Choirboy's ruffle

Stippled icing template

Holly leaf stencil

Peace

Rich colours, traditional decorations and an unusual cake shape all combine to make a stunning example of sugarcraft to impress your Christmas guests.

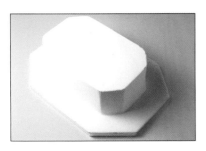

1 Coat a long 23cm (9in) octagonal cake top, sides and board with white royal icing.

2 To make the runout candle, trace the candle outline. Place a piece of waxed paper over the drawing and outline in red icing using a No1 tube. Flood in with red-orange runout icing. Outline and flood in the flame with yellow icing and a No1 tube. Let dry. Reserve some red-orange icing for later use.

3 Paint orange detail on flame with food colouring.

4 Prepare a Christmas rose, a few pine branches, some sugarpaste holly leaves and a marzipan fir cone.

5 Use the reserved red-orange icing to pipe some small bulbs onto waxed paper for the base border decoration. Let dry.

6 Transfer the Christmas scene outline to the cake top and paint with food colouring.

7 Remove the candle from the waxed paper and attach to cake top over the painted scene. Attach runout flame. Pipe the candle wick with black icing using No1 tube.

8 Arrange the piped pine branches, marzipan fir cone, holly leaves, and Christmas rose at the base of the candle. Pipe some red berries using a No1 tube. Complete by brushing on some softened white icing below the candle, and sprinkle with granulated sugar to give a frosty effect.

9 Mark a circle on each of the four sides (not the small corners) and, using a No1 tube and green icing, pipe a wreath of small holly leaves. Pipe a few spikes of green icing to add depth to the wreath, and pipe a few red berries using a No0 tube. Pipe bows onto waxed paper, allow to dry, then lift off and attach to holly wreath.
Use a No3 tube and white icing to pipe a border of bulbs on the top edge and the base of the four sides. Leave to dry.

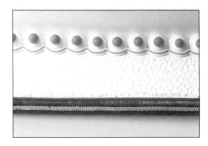

10 Remove red-orange bulbs and attach one to each base bulb with a small dot of icing. Pipe a tapered rope scroll at each base corner. Pipe 2.1. linework on the board to follow the bulb and scroll. Overpipe the top line with green icing using a No1 tube. Complete the board decoration by piping fine filigree using a No1 tube and white icing.

11 For the top border, pipe a continuous line on the edge of the bulbs using a No2 tube and white icing. Overpipe with green icing using a No1 tube. Pipe a line on the cake top to follow the bulbs using a No1 tube and white icing.

12 Pipe two parallel lines on the sides with holly wreaths using a No1 tube and white icing. The lines should go beneath the top bulb border and down each corner edge; curl the inside line at the base. Overpipe the top line in green icing using a No1 tube. The top edges of the four small corners are decorated with icicles piped with a No2 tube and slightly softened white icing. Sprinkle with granulated sugar to give a frosty effect. Remove excess sugar. Add a small gold band. Complete cake by attaching a green and gold ribbon to the board edge.

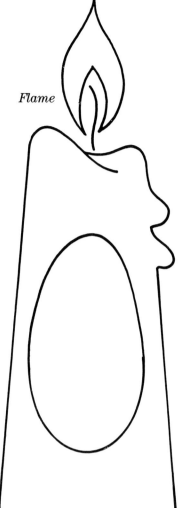

Flame

Outline with red icing

Candle template

Outline for painted scene in candle

Holly wreath size guide

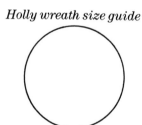

Piped holly wreath

Bow for holly wreath

Poinsettia

*An easy idea for a beginner. Pipe
the shells onto waxed paper and
then assemble to form an
attractive border. The flower could
be modelled from sugarpaste
instead of a runout and painting
as shown.*

1 Coat a 20cm (8in) round cake top, sides and board in cream-coloured icing. For the final side coat use a cut scraper to create three lines as shown. When icing is dry insert narrow red and green ribbons between the grooves, securing with small dots of icing.

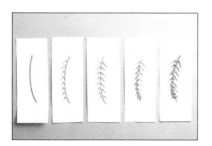

2 Using a No2 tube and chocolate-coloured icing, pipe twigs onto waxed paper. Pipe oval bulbs with red icing for holly berries. Add a small chocolate-coloured icing dot to each berry.

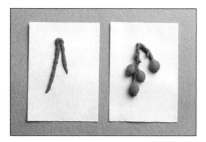

3 Make pine branches using a No1 tube and green icing. Side spikes are pulled out to a point while piping. When dry use a dry brush with edible petal dust, or an aerograph spray to apply brown and green tones.

4 Trace the three poinsettia petals onto drawing paper. Place a piece of waxed paper over the drawing and outline the petals using a No0 tube and white icing. Flood in, place on a curved former and leave to dry. Paint the petals with the same food colouring used on the cake top to ensure a good colour match. Prepare a few runout holly leaves, dried over curved formers.

5 Transfer petal, holly leaf and pine branch outline to cake top. Block in the red and green base colours.

6 Paint shading and detail on petals and leaves using a No1 or No0 paintbrush. Complete with a fine brown outline using a No0 paintbrush.

7 Using small dots of base colour icing, fix runout holly leaves, poinsettia petals and pine branches to lower area of painting.

8 Pipe twig and berries onto top area of painting.

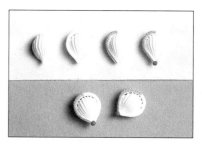

9 To make top and base border decoration, pipe shells onto waxed paper using a No44 tube for top shells and a No32 tube for base shells. Pipe enough shells to fit around the cake. When dry pipe around the shell as shown using a No2 tube for the small shells and a No3 tube for the larger ones. Let dry. Pipe a long roped C-shape around half of each shell using a No1 tube and green icing. Finish each shell with a small red dot using a No1 tube.

Christmas

10 Transfer 'Christmas' inscription to cake top, pipe using a No2 tube and base colour.

11 Overpipe the lettering using a No1 tube and chocolate-coloured icing.

12 Remove shells from waxed paper and attach to cake top edge and base board using small bulbs of icing. Make sure shells are positioned at an angle to the cake as shown. Attach a red velvet ribbon to the cake board edge.

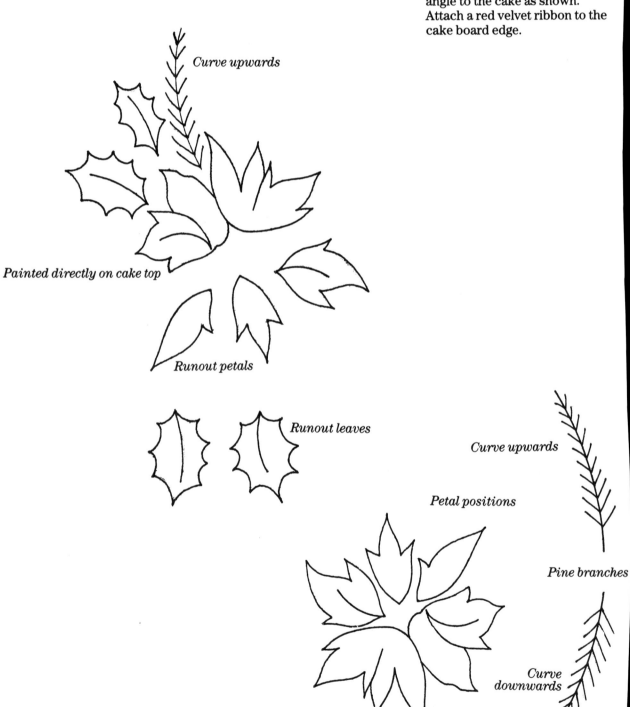

Curve upwards

Painted directly on cake top

Runout petals

Runout leaves

Curve upwards

Petal positions

Pine branches

Curve downwards

34

Noel

*The interesting runout collar
shape on this cake is repeated on
the side and board. Although the
church window looks quite
detailed, it is very easy to achieve.
The gold-edged lettering makes
a nice feature.*

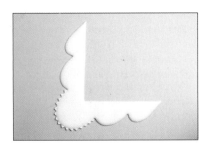

1 Coat a 20cm (8in) square cake top, sides and board with white icing. Make four corner runout collars using the pattern. When dry, use a No1 tube and white icing to pipe a three-dot edging around the curved corner section as shown.

2 To make the choirboy, trace the design onto drawing paper. Position a piece of waxed paper over the design, securing it with dots of icing or small pieces of masking tape. Use a No1 tube with chocolate-coloured icing to pipe all lines, except eyes and details on cassock and surplice. Let dry, then flood in, following the sequence shown, with runout icing. Allow filled in areas to skin over before flooding in adjacent sections. The figure should be a very thin runout figure, without the build-up usually associated with figure piping. As a guide, the thickness of the runout should be the thickness of the tube used for outlining; in this instance, a No1.

3 When completely dry, use food colouring to paint the eye, rosy cheeks and 'Noel' on the hymn sheet with a No0 paintbrush. Use a No1 tube to pipe detail on cassock and surplice with red and white icing as shown. Pipe lace edging on the surplice with a No0 tube and white icing.

4 Trace 'Noel' inscription onto drawing paper or thin card. Tape a piece of waxed paper over the lettering. Outline using a No1 tube and let dry. Carefully paint the lettering outline with edible gold colouring. Leave to dry. Flood in the gold outlines with red runout icing; allow to dry. Do not overfill; make thin runout lettering to match the figure.

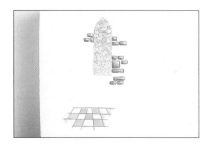

5 Trace the church wall and floor outline and transfer onto the cake top. Paint irregular coloured shapes over the window with food colouring. Paint the stone wall, outlining with a fine brown line. The floor is painted grey, with darker grey lines to represent the tile joins.

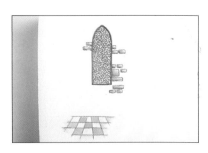

6 Using a No0 tube with chocolate-coloured icing, pipe fine filigree over church window to create a stained glass effect. Outline the window using a No2 tube and chocolate-coloured icing.

7 Remove choirboy from waxed paper and position on three or four small bulbs of icing so he is raised off the cake. Remove 'Noel' lettering from paper and attach to the cake top with dots of white icing.

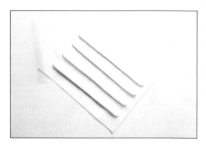

8 Pipe four straight white lines the same length as the depth of the cake onto waxed paper using a No44 tube. Let dry.

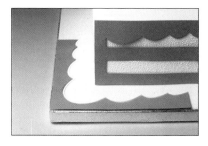

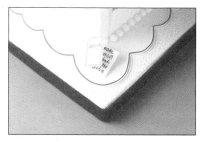

The corners of the cake may also be finished, as shown here, with a carol book and music sheet. Both pieces are cut from white sugarpaste. The book is dried over a folded piece of thin card. Paint the detail with black food colouring using a fine paintbrush.

9 Trace side design template onto thin card or drawing paper, cut out, align against the cake side and secure with masking tape. Pipe filigree using a No1 tube and white icing in cut out sections of the template. Repeat on all four sides.

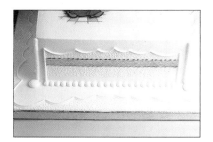

10 Remove the template. Follow curved edge of the filigree with a line piped using a No2 tube and white icing. Use the same tube to pipe vertical lines at each end of the side panels. Secure a strip of 15mm (½in) silver band on each side panel.

11 Decorate the cake board with a design to match the top collar. Trace the corner template onto thin card and cut out. Position template on corner of cake board and pipe 2.1. linework in white alongside it. Repeat on all four corners, finishing the top line in red icing using a No1 tube. Pipe filigree using a No1 tube and white icing in the area between the linework and the cake board edge. Remove piped lines from waxed paper and attach one to each corner of the cake side with white icing. Pipe a bulb at the base of each line, using a No3 tube and slightly softened white icing. Allow bulbs to dry completely. Pipe line and bulb with filigree using a No1 tube and white icing. Remove top collars from waxed paper, position and attach to cake top. Pipe 2.1. linework on cake surface to follow inside edge of collars. Attach a red velvet ribbon to the cake board edge.

Stone wall outline

Church window

Choirboy

Noel

Floor

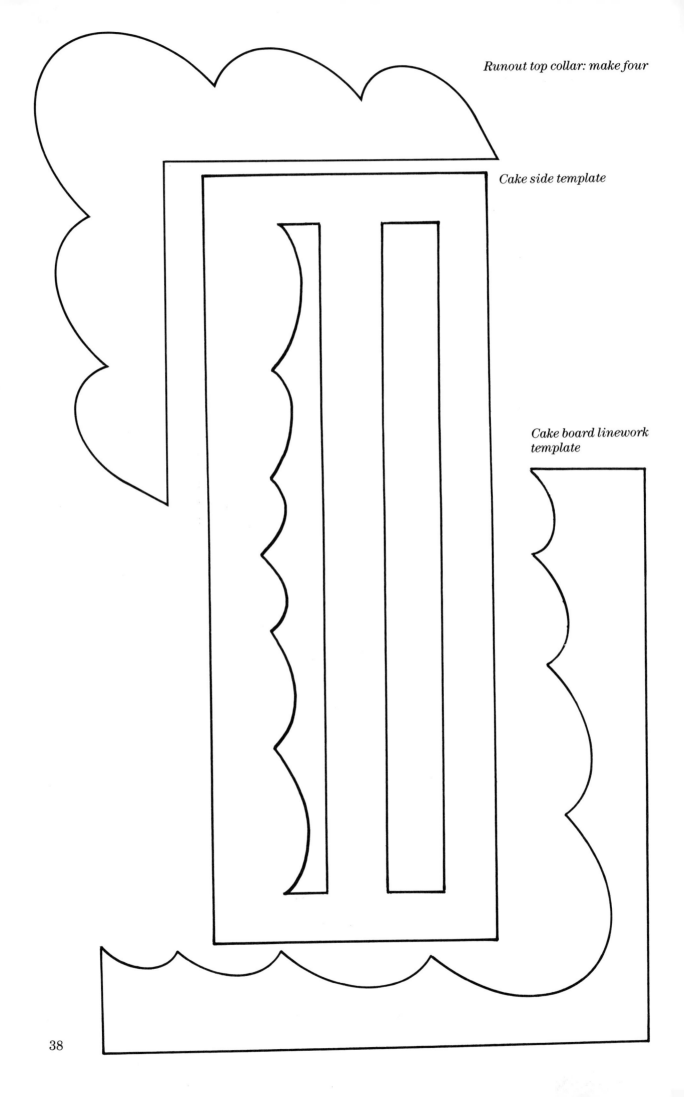

Runout top collar: make four

Cake side template

*Cake board linework
template*

38

Winter Scene

*A minimum amount of piped
decoration emphasizes the smooth
iced surface. The main decoration
is in the painted Christmas scene
on the runout piece, with the
overall design balanced by the
modelled flower and leaves.*

39

1 Coat a 20cm (8in) round cake top, sides and board with peach-coloured icing. Make runout plaque for cake top using drawing. Outline using a No1 tube and white icing, flood in with white runout icing and dry.

2 Make base collar using pattern. Outline using a No1 tube and white icing. Flood in with white runout icing and dry.

3 Prepare a large Christmas rose, a few paste holly leaves and some piped pine branches.

4 Paint Christmas snow scene on plaque using food colouring. Use the picture outline provided, or copy your favourite winter scene. Shade the background with a dry brush and edible petal dust, or use an aerograph. Prepare a card template from the drawing to mask the plaque, leaving the sky area exposed for shading.

5 Remove base collar from waxed paper. Place the collar over the cake and onto the cake board, attaching with icing. Stick a narrow gold ribbon around the base of the cake side; join at the back of the cake.

6 Pipe a small plain shell using a No3 tube and white icing. Edge the shell with a fine chocolate-coloured scratched scallop line using a No1 tube. Pipe 2.1. linework around runout collar edge.

7 Attach a narrow gold band, as used on the base, to the top of the cake side. Join at the back of the cake.

8 Position and attach the plaque. Pipe 2.1. linework around the cake top edge and following the shape of the plaque. Finish with a chocolate-coloured line using a No1 tube.

9 Attach Christmas rose, holly leaves, berries and pine branches in position as shown. Transfer lettering outline onto cake top and pipe using a No2 tube and red icing. Let dry, then overpipe top half of lettering using a No2 tube and white icing to look like fallen snow. Complete with a green velvet ribbon attached to the cake board edge.

Base collar: trace drawings of quarter sections. Join four sections together at A,B,C and D. Use the cake diameter line nearest to the size of fully coated cake. Pipe along this line when making runout.

A

C   D

Cake diameter line

B

Runout plaque for cake top

Outline for painted scene

Happy Christmas

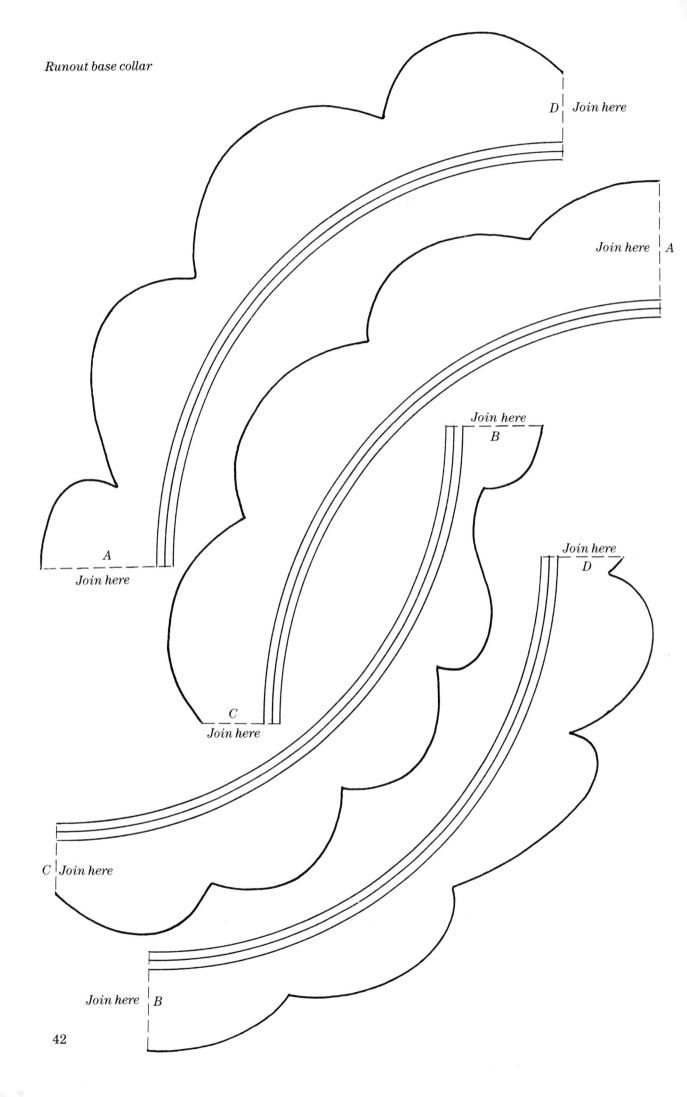

Runout base collar

D | Join here

Join here | A

Join here
B

A
Join here

Join here
D

C
Join here

C | Join here

Join here | B

42

Angel

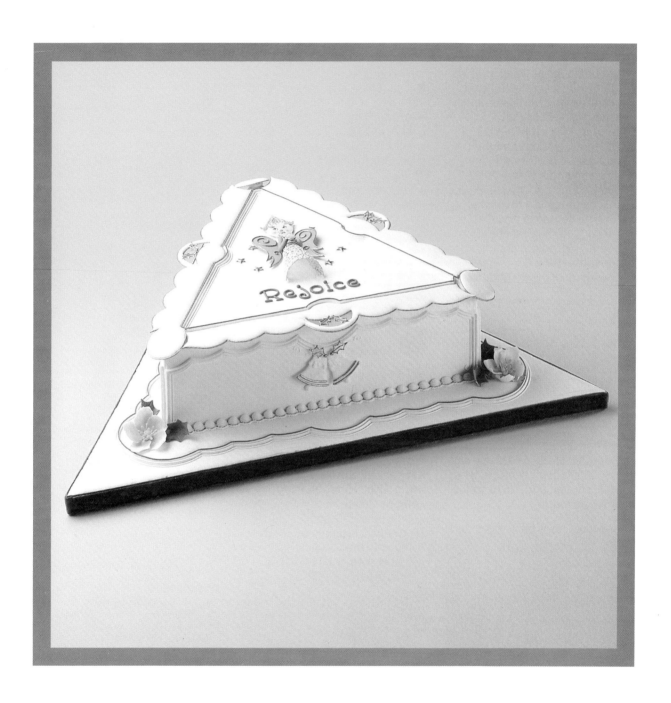

*This triangular-shaped cake is
certain to create a sensation on
any Christmas table. Try a Father
Christmas or snowman with the
cone shaped body, and change the
inscription to suit the figure.*

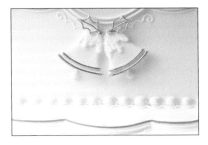

1 Coat a 25cm (10in) triangular cake top, sides and board in ivory-coloured icing. Using the drawing, pipe six outline holly leaves with berries. When dry, paint the leaves and berries with edible gold colouring. Make runout collars with cutout sections and three round discs for the top. Three base runout collars are also required. Pipe the top collars and round discs using a No1 tube. Allow the outline to dry, then paint with edible gold colouring. Flood in with base colour runout icing. Outline and flood in the base collars in base colour icing.

2 To make angel's body, pipe filigree using a No1 tube and blue icing halfway round a lightly greased cream horn tin or trellis former and let dry.

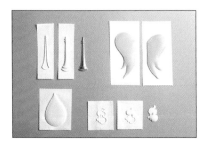

3 Pipe angel's face and hands, outlining with a No1 tube and flesh-coloured icing. Flood in. Pipe wings and horn, painting the horn when dry with edible gold colouring.

4 When runout sections for angel are completely dry, paint eyes, nose and mouth using food colouring. Pipe hair using No1 and No0 tubes. Let dry. Pipe lines onto wings, allow to dry, then carefully paint with edible gold colouring. Prepare some small stencilled stars; paint gold when dry. Pipe the inscription 'Rejoice' onto waxed paper using a No2 tube and copper-coloured icing.

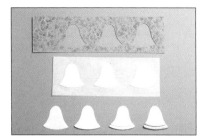

5 Prepare six paste holly leaves and three Christmas roses. Prepare a bell stencil from the template. Make six stencilled bells, following the instructions for stencilled leaves on page 7. When bells are dry, pipe two lines across the base of each using a No2 tube and ivory-coloured icing, let dry. Paint the lines with edible gold colouring. Pipe snow at top of each bell using a No1 tube and white icing. Sprinkle with granulated sugar to create a frosty effect.

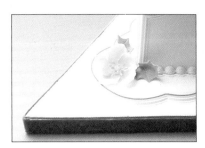

6 Attach base collars to cake board; pipe 3.2.1. linework on the board around collar edge. Overpipe with copper-coloured icing. Prepare a template and use as a guide to pipe 3.2.1. linework on each cake side. Pipe a small,

scratched scallop beneath centre curve. Pipe a small shell using a No42 tube along base of cake side and base collar join. Attach two prepared holly leaves and a Christmas rose at each corner.

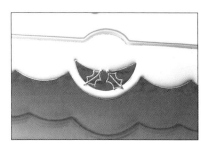

7 Referring to the photo, pipe hammers for bells directly on sides with a No2 tube and ivory icing. Position the bells, attaching with icing. Add two piped holly leaves and berries.

8 Position and attach angel's body, head and wings. Support wings with small pieces of foam until dry. Pipe arms on cake using a No3 tube and coffee-coloured icing. Attach gold horn and hands. Remove lettering from waxed paper and attach to cake top with small dots of ivory icing.

9 When dry, remove collars from waxed paper and attach two gold holly leaves to each cutout section of the top collars.

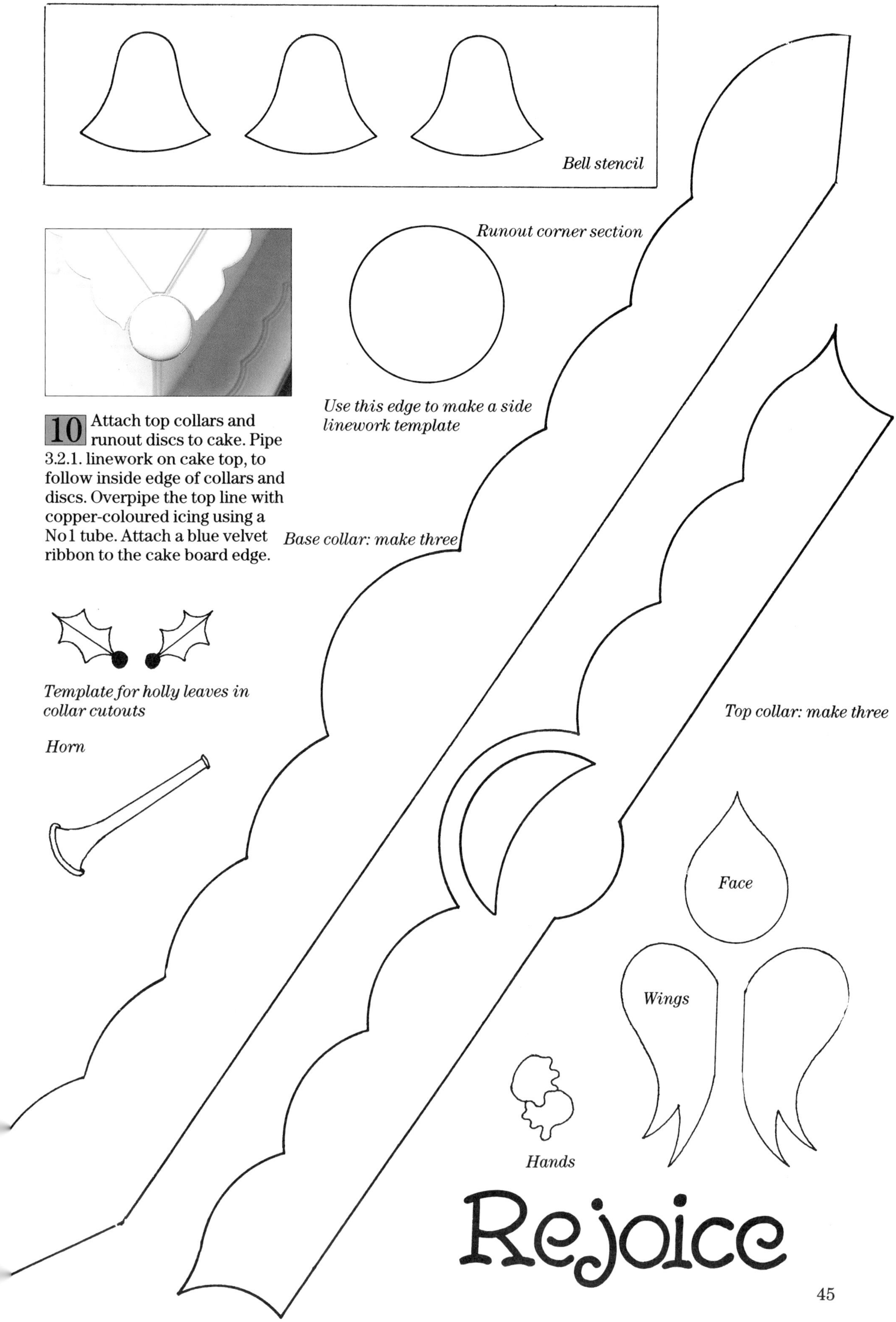

Bell stencil

Runout corner section

Use this edge to make a side linework template

10 Attach top collars and runout discs to cake. Pipe 3.2.1. linework on cake top, to follow inside edge of collars and discs. Overpipe the top line with copper-coloured icing using a No 1 tube. Attach a blue velvet ribbon to the cake board edge.

Base collar: make three

Template for holly leaves in collar cutouts

Horn

Top collar: make three

Face

Wings

Hands

Rejoice

45

Candle

The use of curved, piped holly
leaves complements the stylish
outline of the runout collar. There
are four candle designs to choose
from, which also look nice painted
with gold or silver food colouring.

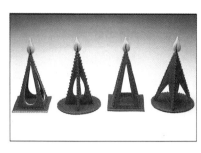

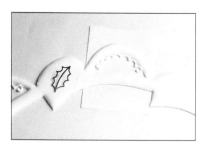

1 Coat a 20cm (8in) round cake top, sides and board with white icing. Make a full runout collar for cake top. Outline using a No1 tube and white icing; flood in. Dry. Pipe outline holly leaves on waxed paper using a No1 tube and green icing. Place in curved formers to dry. Colour with green and brown tones using a dry brush and edible petal dust, or spray food colour with an aerograph.

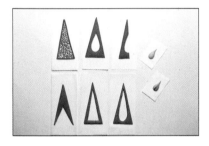

2 Make four runout sides and one base for candle centrepiece. Outline using a No1 tube and red icing, flood in with red runout icing and leave to dry. Make a runout flame in egg-yellow coloured icing. Pipe an elongated bulb onto waxed paper; pull out a point using a fine paintbrush. When dry, paint centre with orange food colouring.

3 Use red icing to assemble candle, supporting with small polystyrene blocks where necessary. Pipe a tiny bulb edging to conceal the joins using a No1 tube and red icing. Four variations of the finished candle are shown.

4 Prepare a template from the collar design. Position the template on the cake board and pipe 3.2.1. linework to match the top collar shape. Finish the top line using a No1 tube and moss green icing.
Pipe a small shell around the base of the cake using a No5 tube and white icing.

5 Pipe detail in cutout sections of collar using a No1 tube and white icing. Attach the holly leaves with tiny lines of white icing. Pipe berries using a No1 tube and red icing. Attach ribbon and bow to the cake side.

6 Fix top collar to cake with white icing. Pipe 3.2.1. linework on cake top to follow the runout edge.

7 Fix candle to centre of cake; pipe 2.1. linework around candle base using white icing. Arrange holly leaves, piped berries and add a marzipan fir cone at base of candle. Attach red and gold ribbon to the cake board edge.

Candle templates: make four of one design

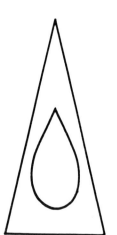

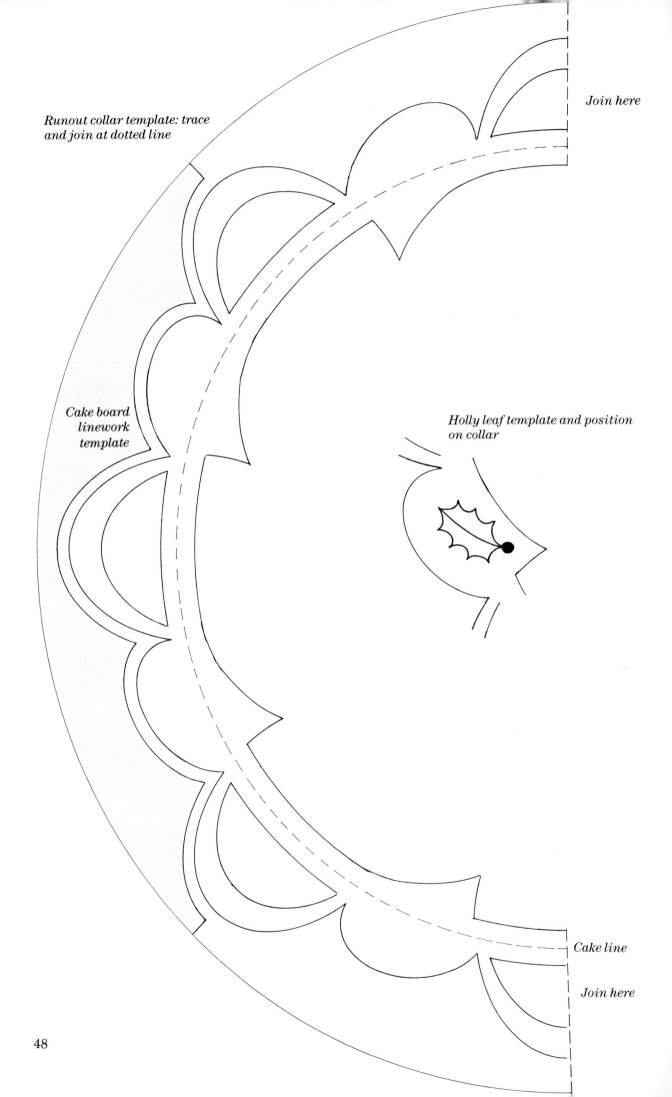

Runout collar template: trace and join at dotted line

Join here

Cake board linework template

Holly leaf template and position on collar

Cake line

Join here

48

Jolly Santa

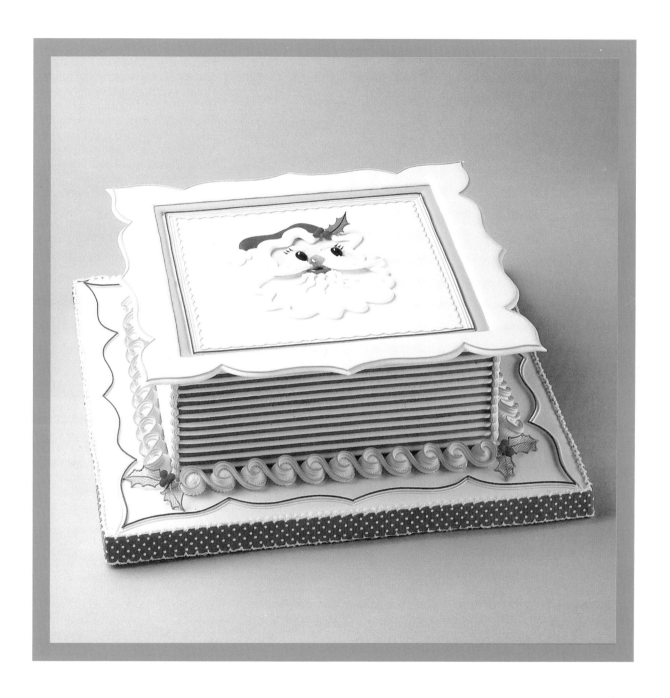

For the more adventurous cake decorator, several piping skills and a double runout collar are used on this cake. Two colours of icing are used with a comb scraper to create the interesting side work.

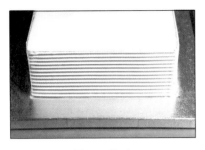

1 Coat a 20cm (8in) square cake with pink icing on the top and chocolate-coloured icing on the sides. Apply a final coat of pink icing to the sides, over the chocolate colour. Use a comb scraper with the tips cut off to reveal the chocolate-coloured icing beneath the pink, creating a two-tone effect. Coat the cake board with pink icing, reserving some for later.

2 Make undercollar from drawing. Use a No1 tube to outline with bright pink icing, flood in with bright pink runout icing and let dry.

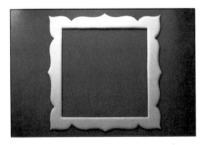

3 Make full runout collar from design. Outline using a No1 tube and base colour pink icing. Flood in and let dry.

4 Trace drawing of Santa's face onto drawing paper or thin card. Position a piece of waxed paper over the drawing,

secure with dots of icing or masking tape. Outline using a No1 tube with red and white icing. The ends of the moustache are piped using a No2 tube to give added stability. Flood in face with red and white runout icing. Beard lines and mouth, moustache and nose, and hat and bobble are flooded separately. Allow each section to skin over before flooding adjacent sections.

5 When eyes are dry, outline eyelids with flesh-coloured icing using a No0 tube. Flood in with flesh colour runout icing. When dry, paint eyes with black food colour and pipe eyelashes using a No0 tube and black icing. Paint nose orange; shade with red. Paint mouth red. Using slightly softened white icing, brush a textured effect on to the moustache and beard line beneath mouth.

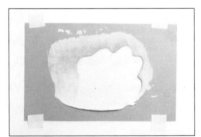

6 Prepare a thin card face stencil from the outline. Align the stencil on the cake top, secure with tape and spread a thin layer of flesh-coloured icing over the cutout area. Remove the stencil. When dry, remove runouts from waxed paper and build up the face on the cake top in the following sequence: hat, hat rim, beard, mouth, moustache, eyes, eyebrows and hat bobble. Attach with dots of icing. Complete hat with a holly leaf and berry.

7 Pipe base border bulbs using a No32 tube and pink icing, overpipe in an S-design using No3 and No2 tubes with pink and No1 tube with bright pink. Prepare a thin card template for the linework. Position on the cake board and outline with 2.1. linework in pink icing. Pipe the top line in chocolate-coloured icing. Pipe a small plain shell with a No1 tube around the board edge. Finish corners with small shell using a No42 tube and pink icing. Attach two tulle holly leaves and red icing berries to corner.

8 Remove the undercollar and top collar from waxed paper. Using a No1 tube and bright pink icing, pipe a line on the surface of the top collar, following the shape of the outside edge, as shown. Leave to dry.

9 Attach undercollar to cake top. Pipe 3.2.1. linework to follow inside edge of undercollar. An advantage of using undercollars is that you can pipe the top linework without the risk of damaging the top collar. Pipe the top line in chocolate-coloured icing using a No1 tube, add a bright pink scratched scallop line.

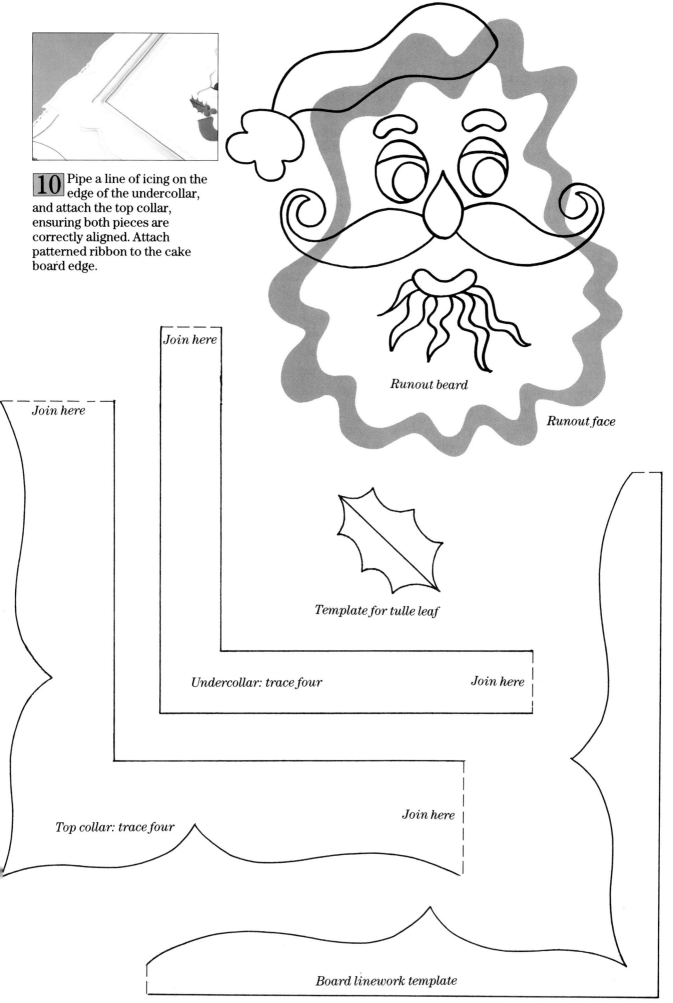

10 Pipe a line of icing on the edge of the undercollar, and attach the top collar, ensuring both pieces are correctly aligned. Attach patterned ribbon to the cake board edge.

Runout beard

Runout face

Join here

Join here

Template for tulle leaf

Undercollar: trace four

Join here

Top collar: trace four

Join here

Board linework template

Midnight

This cute little owl stands out well
on the black background. The
white runout collars and linework
create a crisp appearance.
If you find lettering difficult,
simply position the owl in the
centre of the cake.

52

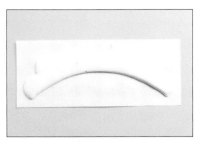

1 Coat a 20cm (8in) round cake; top, sides and board in black royal icing. Make top and base collar runouts. Outline using a No1 tube and white icing, flood in with white runout icing, allow to dry. When top runouts are completely dry, pipe a three-dot edging on the outside edge of the centre curved sections.

2 Make owl motif. Trace, then outline using a No1 tube.

3 Flood in as shown in sequence here allowing each section to skin over before flooding adjacent sections. Dry.

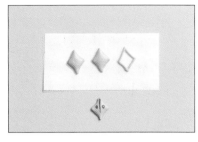

4 The beak is outlined using a No0 tube and egg-yellow coloured icing, flood in. Let dry. When dry, paint detail on using food colouring.

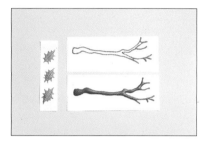

5 Pipe branch. Outline using a No1 tube and chocolate-coloured icing, flood in. Allow to dry.

6 Thinly brush the fur rim and bobble of the hat with slightly softened white icing. Sprinkle with granulated sugar while still wet, then brush off excess sugar. Paint eyes on owl using food colouring. Attach beak.

7 Attach base runouts to cake board, filling the space between the cake and runout with white icing. Pipe small white bulbs along the join against the cake side using a No2 tube. Pipe 3.2.1. linework on the cake board, alongside the runout edge.

8 With small bulbs of icing, attach the branch, owl and owl's tail beneath the branch. Pipe claws on branch using a No2 tube and egg-yellow coloured icing. Pipe snow along top of branch using a No1 tube and white icing, sprinkle with granulated sugar, then remove excess sugar. Attach a few prepared snowballs; these are small granulated sugar-sprinkled white icing bulbs, piped onto waxed paper and allowed to dry.

9 Pipe lettering using a No1 tube and red icing; use a template if necessary. Attach a narrow silver band around the side of the cake. Remove top collar runouts from waxed paper, position and attach to the cake top. Pipe 3.2.1. linework to follow the inside edge of the collars, joining at the space between the sections.

10 Arrange and attach two piped holly leaves in each space between the base runouts. Pipe on holly berries using a No1 tube and red icing. Attach a black velvet ribbon to the cake board edge.

Runout base collar: make four

Runout top collar: make four

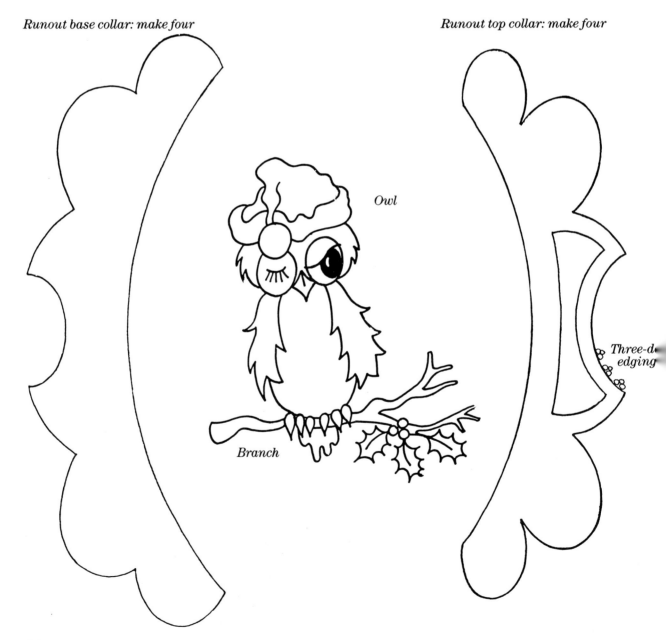

Owl

Three-d・ edging

Branch

Lantern

An interesting use of chocolate-coloured outlines emphasizes the lively runout collar shapes. The greetings inscription has been designed to match the collar shape.

1 Coat a 20cm (8in) square cake top, sides and board with lemon-coloured icing. For the final side coating use a cut scraper to create a combed texture on the lower half. Make four top corner runout collars; using a No1 tube outline all lines in base colour icing except the outside curved edges which are outlined in chocolate-coloured icing. Flood in with base colour runout icing.

2 Make four base corner runout collars. Outline using a No1 tube and base colour icing, flood in and let dry. Make four side corner sections; outline the two straight sides in base colour icing, and the curved edges in chocolate-coloured icing, using a No1 tube. Flood in; let dry. Remove the side corner sections from waxed paper, turn over and repeat outlining and flooding in. Allow to dry.

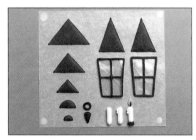

3 Make runout pieces for lantern. The window sections are piped directly onto pieces of leaf gelatine, cut to the correct size and shape from the drawing. The candle is piped using a No4 tube and white icing. Pipe two tiny bulbs to represent running wax. Using a No1 tube

and chocolate-coloured icing pipe three lines around the base of the candle, to form a holder. The flame can be piped in yellow icing, or in white icing and painted yellow with food colour when dry. Pipe or paint the black candle wick. Allow to dry.

4 Trace inscription 'Greetings' onto drawing paper. Place a piece of waxed paper over the drawing and outline with a No1 tube for the sections to be flooded, and a No2 tube for the single strokes. Flood in with green runout icing. When dry, apply green shading using petal dust or an aerograph.

5 Assemble lantern using chocolate-coloured icing; let dry. Leave brown, or paint gold. Colour a small area of the cake top yellow. Fix the piped candle in position. Position and attach the lantern. Pipe branches using a No1 tube and chocolate icing. Pipe holly leaves and berries onto the branches. A few holly leaves, piped onto waxed paper and allowed to dry, could be attached to give more depth. Complete the lantern by piping on white icing and sprinkling with granulated sugar to create a frosty effect. Attach a tiny red ribbon bow. Remove lettering from waxed paper, position and attach to cake top with small dots of base colour icing.

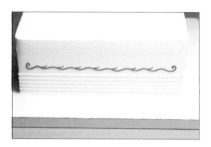

6 For the side decoration, pipe a wavy chocolate-coloured line along each side, just above the comb scraping. Follow the drawing for the wavy line. Pipe holly leaves and berries.

7 Fix base collars and side corner sections using base colour icing. Where the base collar joins the cake side, pipe a small shell using a No3 tube, then pipe a small shell down each corner section using a No42 tube; use base colour for shells.

8 Pipe 3.2.1. linework on the cake board alongside the runout edge. Pipe the top line in chocolate-coloured icing using a No1 tube.

9 Attach top collars. Pipe 3.2.1. linework on cake surface around inside edge of collars. Pipe the top line in chocolate-coloured icing using a No1 tube. Attach a gold ribbon to the board.

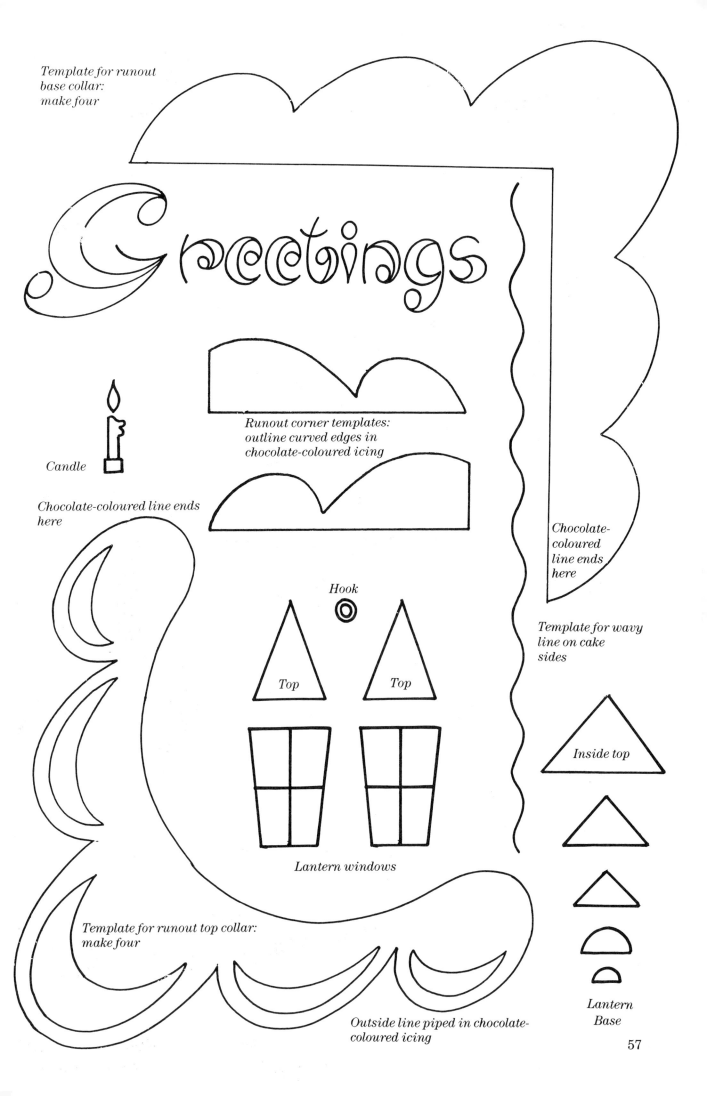

Template for runout base collar: make four

Candle

Chocolate-coloured line ends here

Greetings

Runout corner templates: outline curved edges in chocolate-coloured icing

Chocolate-coloured line ends here

Template for wavy line on cake sides

Hook

Top

Top

Inside top

Lantern windows

Lantern Base

Template for runout top collar: make four

Outside line piped in chocolate-coloured icing

57

Carol

The interesting use of stencils provides an attractive cake side frieze. If you prefer, the lamp post could be made as a runout, like the carol singer, to eliminate the need for painting directly onto the cake surface.

1 Coat a 20cm (8in) round cake top, sides and board with white icing. Make runout collars for top and base. Trace the drawings, place a piece of waxed paper over the tracing and outline with white icing using a No1 tube. Flood in with white runout icing. Dry.

2 Prepare eight small icing bells; pipe a white drop with a bulb on top on waxed paper, using a No2 tube. Allow the surface to crust over, then carefully scoop out the soft centre using a small paintbrush. Dry. Paint gold.

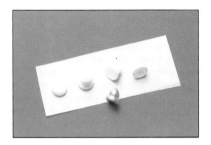

3 Pipe some small icing bulbs of various colours onto waxed paper with No1 tube. Dry.

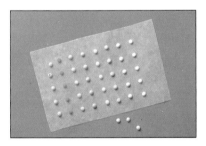

4 To make the runout figure, trace the outline onto drawing paper. Place a piece of waxed paper over the tracing and outline using a No1 tube.

How to make side tree stencil
Drawing 1
Cut a length of cartridge paper to fit exactly around your prepared, coated cake. The paper strip should also be the height of the cake side.

Drawing 2
With the paper strip flat, accurately measure and divide the length into four equal sections. Trace the tree design provided into each of the four sections, ensuring that the trees are centrally positioned in each section.

Drawing 3
Cut out each tree shape with a sharp craft knife. The stencil is now ready for use.

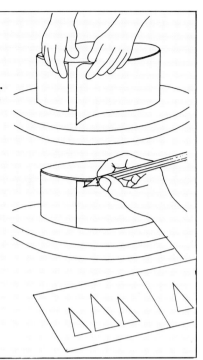

5 Flood in each section separately. Allow sections to skin over before flooding in adjacent sections.

6 Continue flooding in until the figure is complete. Let dry.

7 Paint detail on the figure with a fine paintbrush and food colouring.

8 Prepare a side template for the stencils. Secure to cake with masking tape. Colour the trees green by brushing edible petal dust over the cut areas or by spreading green royal icing over the template. The cake top and base board should be masked off to prevent marking. Remove the template.

9 Cut a thin card template for the cake side linework; attach to cake side with masking tape and pipe 2.1. linework next to it. Repeat around the cake. Remove icing bulbs from paper and attach to the Christmas trees with icing.

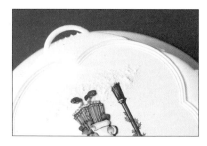

10 Remove collars from waxed paper. Attach base collars with icing, centring them beneath the Christmas tree panels. Use a No2 tube and slightly softened white icing to pipe bulbs, graduating in size, along the join of the runout to the cake side. Pipe 3.2.1. linework on the cake board next to the runout edge. The spaces between the collars are joined with semi-circles.

11 Transfer the lantern outline onto the cake top. Paint with food colouring using a fine paintbrush. The yellow glow around the top of the lamp may be painted on with a fine paintbrush, or use an aerograph. Slightly soften some white icing and partly mix in a small amount of blue colouring. Brush around the base of the lamp and sprinkle with granulated sugar. Remove excess sugar.

12 Remove the figure from the waxed paper and attach beside the lamp. Finish the top collars by piping a three-dot pattern in the cutout sections using a No1 tube and white icing. Attach two gold icing bells to each collar section and pipe the holly leaves and berries using a No1 tube. Attach the collars to the cake top with icing, centred over the Christmas tree panels. Pipe white 3.2.1. linework next to collars. Attach a green and gold velvet ribbon to the cake board edge.

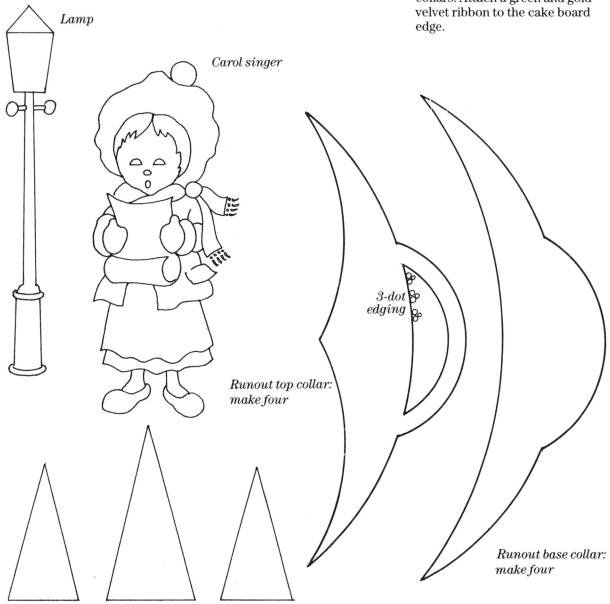

Lamp

Carol singer

3-dot edging

Runout top collar: make four

Runout base collar: make four

Tree stencil

Silent Night

*The clever design of these corner
runout collars with overlays,
creates the illusion of a full collar.
The shepherd figure could be a
runout on waxed paper instead of
being painted directly onto the
cake surface.*

1 Coat a 20cm (8in) square cake top, sides and board with white icing. The final coat of icing on the sides is finished using a scraper cut as shown to make four lines. Make top and base runout collars; four sections for each. Make runout overlay pieces; four for the top and four for the base. Outline all sections in white icing using a No1 tube, flood in and dry.

2 When top collars are completely dry, remove from waxed paper. Use top collar drawing as a guide to pipe filigree onto waxed paper using a No1 tube and white icing. Pipe a line of icing attached to the edge of the filigree work with a No1 tube; immediately position the collar section onto the filigree. Carefully slide a thin knife blade between the drawing and the waxed paper, then gently lift and secure paper and filigree to the underside of the runout section. Remove knife and let dry.

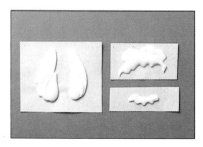

3 Make runout pieces for sleeves, gown collar and headdress. Outline each using a No1 tube, flood in separate sections using white runout icing. Allow sections to skin over before flooding adjacent ones.

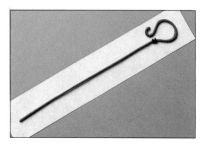

4 Pipe crook onto waxed paper using a No2 tube and chocolate-coloured icing. Pipe detail on using a No1 tube.

5 Trace 'Silent Night' onto drawing paper, secure a piece of waxed paper over the lettering and pipe using a No2 tube and pale blue icing. When dry shade lettering a darker blue colour at the base, fading towards the middle.

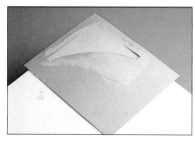

6 Prepare a corner stencil from thin card. Position the template on a corner of cake top, hold firmly and spread a small amount of coffee-coloured icing over the cutout area. Spread evenly in one complete motion. Remove template and repeat on each corner. Leave to dry.

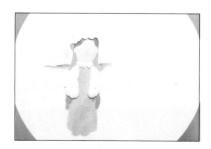

7 Transfer background scene and outline of figure to cake top. Paint in the basic areas of colour. Attach pieces.

8 Outline figure with a fine line of black food colouring using a No0 paintbrush. Pipe the stars using a No0 tube and white icing. When dry paint with edible silver colouring. Remove crook from waxed paper and attach to the figure with icing. Pipe hands using No2 tube and flesh-coloured icing. Carefully remove lettering from waxed paper, position on cake top and secure with tiny dots of icing.

9 Remove base collars from waxed paper, position and secure on cake board with white icing. Fill in the space between the cake side and runout with white icing. Attach base collar overlays to cover ends of collar. Pipe a small plain shell using a No2 tube and white icing along the bottom of each cake side, omitting overlay area. Pipe 2.1. linework on cake board to follow collar. Pipe top line using a No1 tube and coffee-coloured icing. Attach a narrow silver cake band to each side, between the two scraper lines. Attach two paste holly leaves and a small marzipan fir cone to the base collar at each corner. Gently remove paper from filigree sections on top collars, taking care not to damage the filigree. Attach the top collars to the cake, then position and secure overlay pieces. Pipe 2.1. linework on the cake surface to follow inside edge of collar and overlay. Pipe top line using a No1 tube and coffee coloured icing. A coffee-coloured velvet ribbon attached to the cake board edge completes the cake.

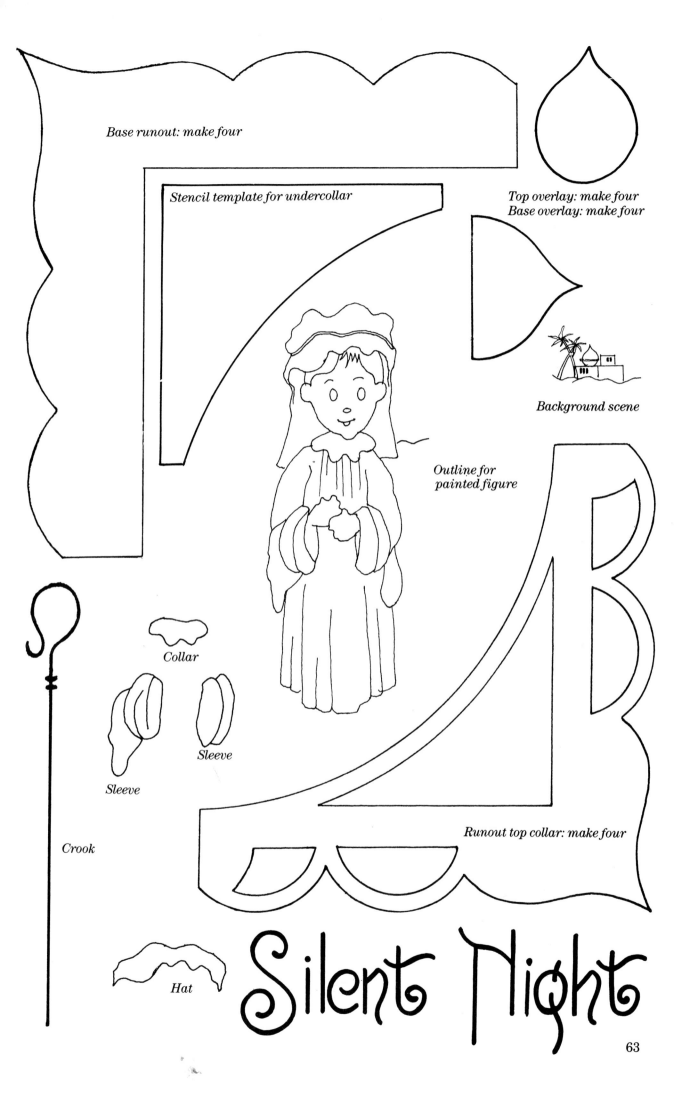

Base runout: make four

Stencil template for undercollar

Top overlay: make four
Base overlay: make four

Background scene

Outline for
painted figure

Collar

Sleeve

Sleeve

Runout top collar: make four

Crook

Hat

Silent Night

Christmas Eve

A cuddly teddy bear and detailed patchwork quilt make a lovely centrepiece for this unusually-shaped cake. Fancy runout sections make good use of the cut-off corners.

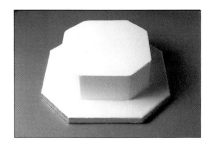

1 Coat a 20cm (8in) square-octagonal cake top, sides and board with white icing.

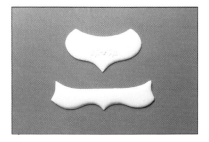

2 To make the collars for the cake top, use the outlines given to make four runouts of each design. Place waxed paper over the templates and outline using a No1 tube. Flood in with white runout icing and let dry. Pipe the holly and berry design onto the corner runouts using a No1 tube and white icing. If necessary trace the holly design onto the runout first.

3 To make teddy in bed, trace outline onto drawing paper. Place a piece of waxed paper over the drawing, outline using a No1 tube and coloured icings as shown. The bed posts are piped in white icing using a No3 tube. Pipe a few bulbs on the bed cover to create extra relief.

Window scene   *Window frame*

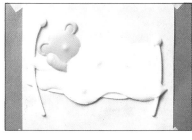

4 Flood in the outlines with coloured runout icing, allowing individual sections to skin over before flooding adjacent sections. Allow to dry.

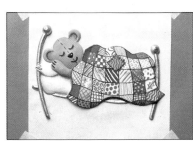

5 Paint bed posts with edible gold colouring. Paint the patchwork quilt with a variety of patterns and colours.

6 Outline a pair of slippers using a No1 tube, and flood in. Use the drawing as a template. When dry, paint on the detail with food colouring and pipe on a bobble with white icing and a No1 tube.

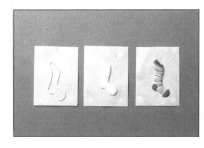

7 Outline five stockings using a No1 tube, and flood in. Allow to dry. Paint on detail with food colouring.

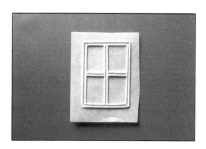

8 Use the same method to make the window frame.

9 Transfer the candlestick and window scene outline onto the cake top. Paint the scene using food colouring. The candlestick is piped onto the surface using chocolate-coloured icing and a No1 tube. Pipe the candle with white icing and a No3 tube. The flame is piped with yellow icing and a No1 tube. Paint, brush petal dust or use an aerograph spray over a round stencil to make a glow around the flame. Remove the window frame and teddy in bed from the paper and attach to the cake top with icing.

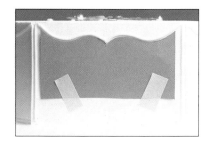

10 Prepare a card template of the side linework outline. Attach to the cake side with masking tape. Outline using white icing and a No2 tube. Remove the template and repeat on all sides.

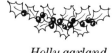

Holly garland

65

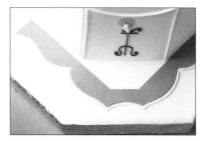

11 Make a template or trace the two curved lines onto each side and using the method for piped holly leaves, pipe the holly garlands with green icing and a No1 tube. Repeat on all sides; finish with small red icing berries and attach a runout stocking with a little icing. Repeat the piped candlestick on each of the corner side panels.

12 The linework for the corners is a scallop at the top and two vertical lines piped with a No2 tube and white icing. Overpipe all side linework with a No1 tube and white icing, then pipe a No1 line inside all lines. Make a card template and use on each of the four board corners to pipe 2.1. linework with white icing. Pipe a scallop along the

edge with chocolate-coloured icing and a No1 tube. Complete the board by piping a rope scroll around the base using a No44 tube and white icing. Remove the collars from the paper and attach to the cake top with icing. Pipe white 2.1. linework to follow the inside edge of collars. Attach red and gold ribbon to the cake board edge.

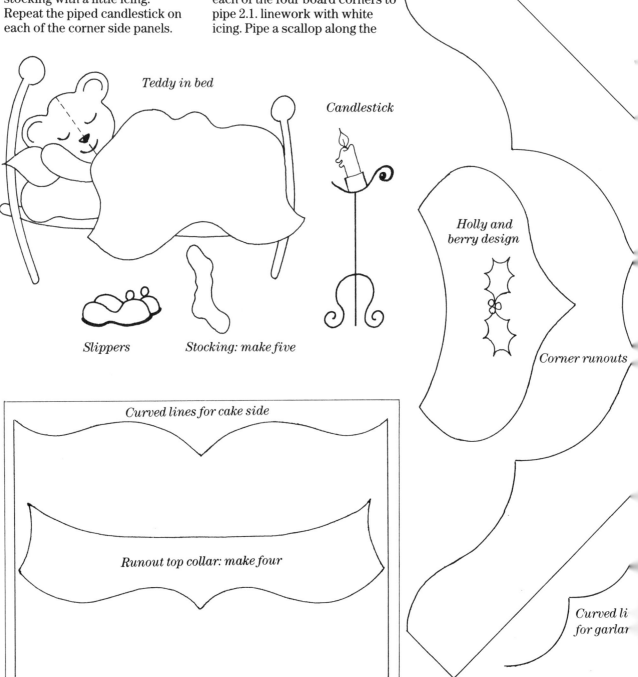

Teddy in bed

Candlestick

Slippers   *Stocking: make five*

Holly and berry design

Corner runouts

Board linework template

Curved lines for cake side

Runout top collar: make four

Curved li for garlar

Holy Night

*Oval shapes piped onto waxed
paper are used to create the stylish
border on this cake. An
experienced sugarcraft enthusiast
will enjoy creating the piped and
painted stable scene.*

1 Coat a 25cm (10in) oval cake top, sides and board with white icing. For the final side coating use a cut scraper to create four lines. To prepare the off pieces for the top and base border, trace the ovals onto drawing paper. The small ovals are for the top edge and the large ones are for the base. Place a piece of waxed paper over the ovals and outline in white icing using a No1 tube. Flood in with white runout icing. Make enough pieces to fit the cake. Dry.

2 To make the stable, thinly roll out some straw-coloured sugarpaste. Cut out the roof using a card template prepared from the drawing. Place over a rounded object, such as the outside of an Easter egg mould. Position roof so that the plain edge will come into contact with the cake surface. Dry.

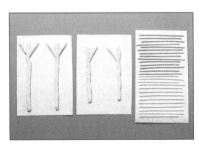

3 To make the straw, pipe lines onto waxed paper using a No1 tube with straw – and coffee-coloured icing. Leave to dry. Pipe the wooden joists on waxed paper using a No2 tube and straw-coloured icing. Use the drawings to make templates. Texture the icing with a fine paintbrush. Let dry.

4 Remove the piped straw from the paper and lightly break into smaller pieces. Brush the stable roof with softened straw-coloured icing and sprinkle with the straw pieces. Remove any excess straw for later use. Paint the joists with orange-brown and egg-yellow food colouring.

5 Transfer the stable scene to the cake top and paint with food colouring. Apply background colouring with a dry brush and petal dust.

6 Remove the roof from the mould and the joists from the waxed paper. Position on cake top and attach with royal icing. Pipe a few tiny bulbs and a star with white icing and a No0 tube. Let dry. Paint with edible silver colouring. Brush a little icing around the stable floor and sprinkle with the reserved straw pieces. Remove excess.

7 Remove border ovals from the waxed paper and attach them all at the same angle to the cake top edge and the base, resting each one on a small bulb of icing. Allow to dry. Using a No2 tube pipe a white line around the edge of the top border. Repeat on the cake board, using a No3 tube, adjacent to the edge of the ovals.

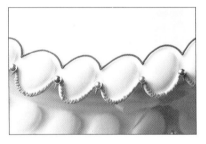

8 Overpipe the top edge line with a fine rope of blue icing using a No1 tube. Pipe a pulled out bulb of copper-coloured icing between each one and add a silver dragée. Complete border by piping a white scallop on the cake top, adjacent to the oval edges, using a No1 tube. Overpipe with chocolate-coloured icing and a No0 tube.

Figure outline

9 For the base, overpipe the line on the board with a rope of white icing using a No2 tube; attach a silver dragée between each oval. Pipe 2.1. linework on the cake board, following the edge of the ovals. Overpipe in blue icing using a No1 tube. Use chocolate-coloured icing and a No1 tube to pipe a scratched scallop on the base board edge. Attach a white satin ribbon and bow to the side, between the scraper lines.

10 Transfer the inscription 'Holy Night' to the cake top and pipe with white icing using a No1 tube. Overpipe using a No1 tube and copper-coloured icing. Attach a blue ribbon to the cake board edge.

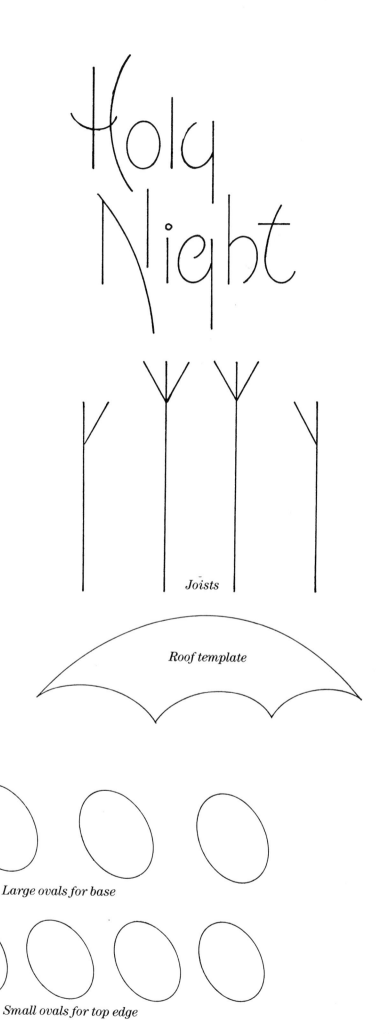

Joists

Roof template

Large ovals for base

Small ovals for top edge

Silhouette

*The sparkle of gold with
traditional red and green on black
and white makes this design an
elegant and unusual feature for
your festive table.*

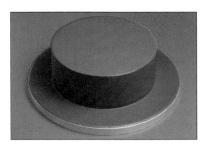

1 Coat a 20cm (8in) round cake top, sides and board in black royal icing.

2 To prepare full runout collar for cake top, outline in white using a No1 tube. Flood in and dry. Take care when removing runout from the waxed paper as it is particularly fragile.

3 For the holly wreath centrepiece, prepare several small sugarpaste holly leaves and 12 small marzipan fir cones. Make some small piped pine branches following the sequence shown for the Poinsettia cake, but make them smaller. Use the drawing as a guide.

4 The gold baubles in the holly wreath are icing bulbs piped onto waxed paper and dried. Paint with edible gold colouring.

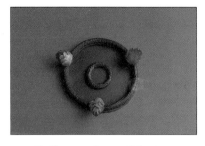

5 Roll out a disc of black sugarpaste approximately 5cm (2in) in diameter. Let dry. Using a No44 tube and black royal icing, pipe a circle around the edge of the disc, followed by a smaller circle in the centre to hold the candle. Leave to dry. Attach three marzipan pine cones with a little black icing.

6 Arrange and attach the pine branches, sugarpaste holly leaves, gold baubles and three more cones to the black icing circle. Attach a gold band to the side of the cake; fix a narrow red ribbon over the gold.

7 To decorate the cake board; prepare a thin card or drawing paper template and position it on the board. Pipe white 3.2.1. linework following the outline. Pipe a white wavy line around the edge using a No1 tube. Fix two sugarpaste holly leaves and piped red berries in the six curved lines. Attach the top collar to cake with short lines of icing.

8 Pipe filigree as shown, between the collar curves and down onto the cake side, using a No0 tube and bright Christmas red icing. Use curved template. Position the holly wreath and finish with a small red candle attached with icing. Attach a red velvet ribbon to the cake board edge.

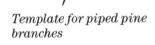

Template for piped pine branches

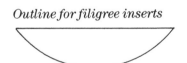

Outline for filigree inserts

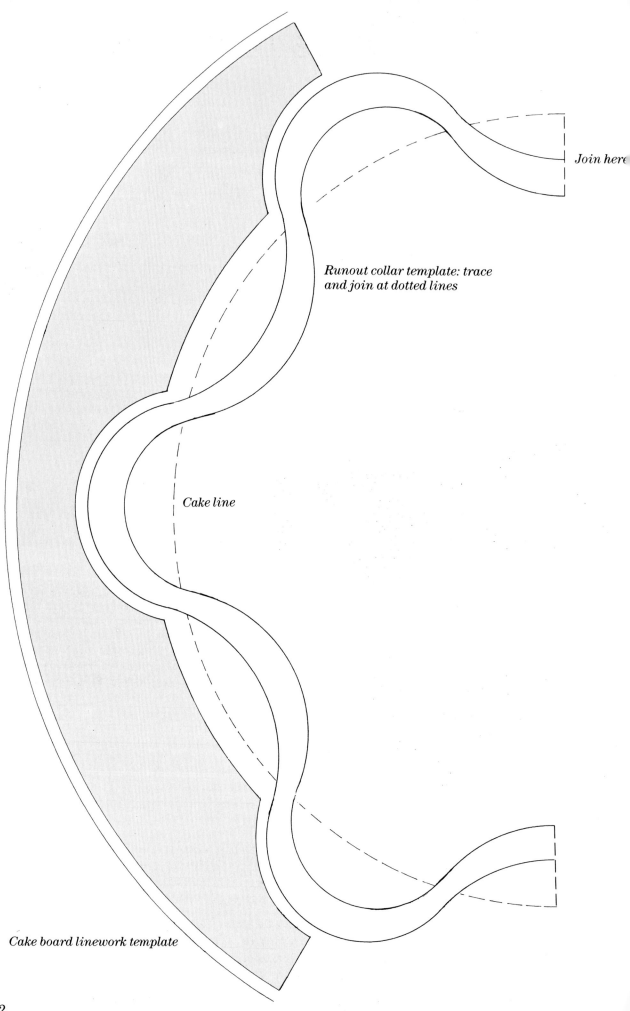

Join here

Runout collar template: trace
and join at dotted lines

Cake line

Cake board linework template

Three Kings

The Three Kings are traced from the template and painted directly onto the cake surface. You could adapt a Christmas card for a different design.

1 Coat a 20cm (8in) square cake top, sides and board with pale green icing. Pipe crowns using No1 and No2 tubes as shown. Place onto 3cm (1½in) curved formers to dry, securing with dots of icing or masking tape. When dry, paint with gold edible food colouring.

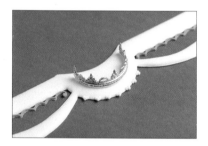

2 Prepare four runout top collars. Outline using a No1 tube and pale green icing, flood in. Allow to dry. Using a No1 tube and coffee-coloured icing, pipe a scalloped line in each cutout section, ensuring that the line is well attached to the runout edge. Pipe a three-dot edging on the curved centre section of the collar edge. Attach prepared gold crowns with a thin line of pale green icing.

3 Make four corner runout pieces. Using a No1 tube, outline the shape on waxed paper, flood in and allow to dry. Repeat outline on reverse side and flood in. Pipe a three-dot edging along the curved edges.

4 Transfer the drawing of the kings onto the cake top. Paint the figures using edible food colourings. First block in the basic colours along with the gold and silver of the crowns and gifts.

5 Paint on the details and features. Complete with a fine black or chocolate-coloured outline.

6 Prepare the side linework template. Cut out the template from thin card or drawing paper, position against the cake side and pipe a line to follow the shape as shown. Use a No2 tube with base green-coloured icing.

7 Remove the template, then pipe a line with a No1 tube alongside the No2 line. Complete sides with a scratched scalloped line next to the No1 line. Attach a strip of narrow gold band. Prepare a template for the board linework design. Position the template on the cake board and pipe 2.1. linework onto the coated board. Pipe a small plain shell along the base of each side with a No3 or No4 tube.

8 Attach top collars and corner sections with base green-coloured icing. Pipe 3.2.1. linework onto cake surface, parallel to inside edge of runout collar. Attach a silver star above the Kings, pipe onto waxed paper using the template. Allow to dry and then paint with silver edible food colouring.

Piped crowns

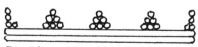

Pipe two lines using No2 tube

Pipe dots using No1 tube

Pipe loops using No1 tube

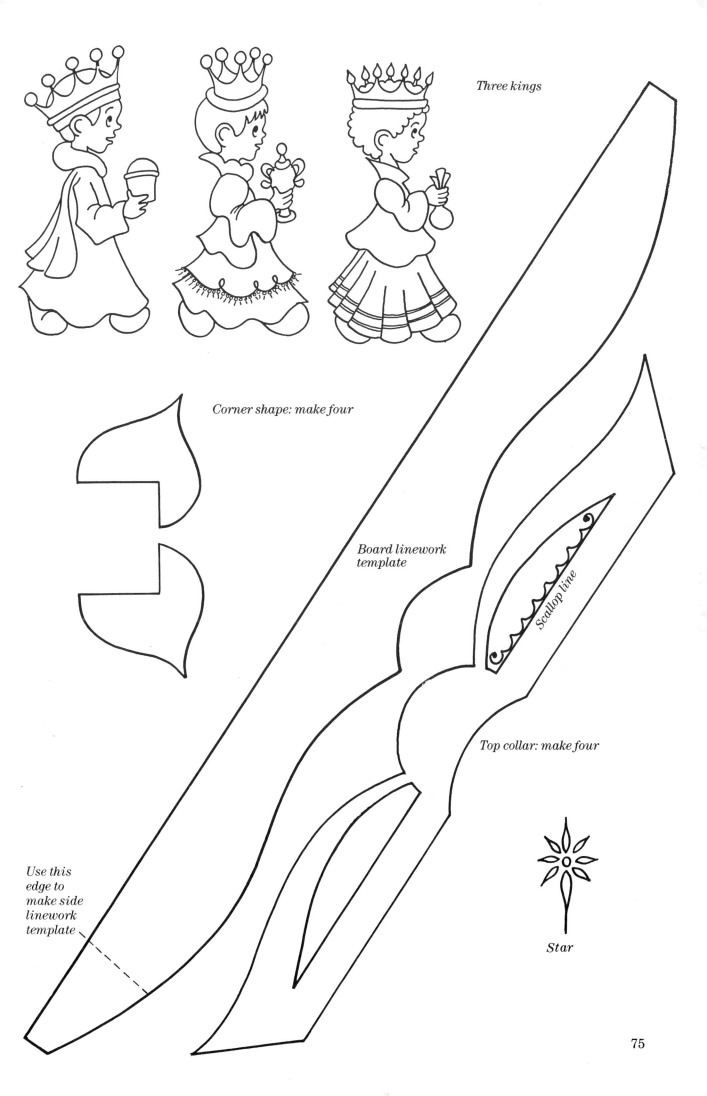

Three kings

Corner shape: make four

Board linework
template

Scallop line

Top collar: make four

Use this
edge to
make side
linework
template

Star

Happy Days

Use your own favourite happy day
memories for the painted side
panels. This elaborate design
involves several sugarcraft skills,
including piping, runout work
and painting. The candle
centrepiece could be replaced by a
piped inscription.

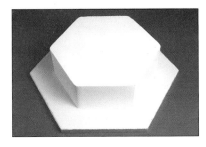

1 Coat a 23cm (9in) hexagonal cake top and sides with white icing. Coat the cake board with pale green icing.

2 Make six runout side panels; tracing the panel outline onto drawing paper. Place a piece of waxed paper over the tracing and outline in white using a No1 tube. Flood in with white runout icing and let dry.

3 Use the panel template for the filigree. Place a piece of waxed paper over the drawing and pipe filigree using a No1 tube and pale green icing. Immediately place a side panel over the filigree and secure with gentle pressure. Let dry. Remove paper and pipe a three-dot edging on the curved section as shown. Repeat for remaining five panels. Prepare 18 paste holly leaves, seven stencilled Christmas roses, piped pine branches and a small marzipan fir cone. Pipe six white icing lines the length of the cake height using a No44 tube. These lines will be used to conceal the joins of the side panels when in position.

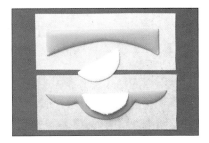

4 Make six runout collar sections for the cake top and six for the base. Prepare templates from the collar outlines. Place a piece of waxed paper over the drawings and outline using a No1 tube and coffee-coloured icing. Flood in with coffee-coloured runout icing. Let dry. Pipe six white semi-circles using a No1 tube. When dry brush the white runout sections with slightly softened white icing; sprinkle with granulated sugar. Attach a runout section to each base collar section.

5 Make six runout overlay sections for the top collars; prepare a template from the outline provided. Place a piece of waxed paper over the pattern and outline with white icing using a No1 tube. Flood in with white runout icing and let dry. Transfer the holly motif onto three of the overlays, and the mistletoe motif onto the remaining three. Paint with a fine paintbrush and food colouring.

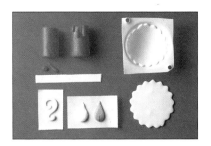

6 To make the candle, roll out some white sugarpaste until quite thin. Cut out a fluted circle from the template and place into a curved former or a section from a plastic fruit tray. Allow to dry. Model the candle from red marzipan, attaching some extra pieces to represent running wax. Attach a narrow strip of white sugarpaste to the base of the candle to form the holder. Pipe handle in white icing using a No3 tube. Pipe a yellow flame onto waxed paper.

7 When dry stick handle to the fluted base, then attach the candle. Paint all white parts with edible gold colouring. Attach flame with icing.

8 Transfer a scene drawing onto each of the six sides, using the template provided to centre them. Paint with food colouring using a fine paintbrush.

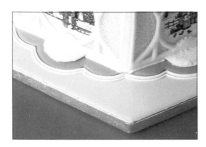

9 Attach the runout side panels with icing; seal the joins with white icing. Attach the prepared white lines to the joins. Attach the base collars with icing and pipe 3.2.1. linework to follow the edge.

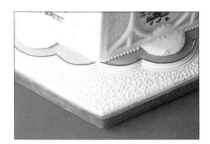

10 Pipe the top line in chocolate-coloured icing using a No 1 tube. Pipe white filigree onto the cake board between linework and the cake board edge. Complete decoration by attaching two paste holly leaves and a Christmas rose at each corner.

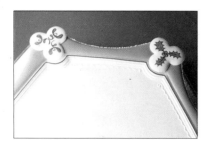

11 Attach the top collar sections to the cake with icing, then attach the overlay pieces to cover the joins. Alternate the overlays with holly and mistletoe designs. Pipe small white icicles on the edge of the top collar using a No 1 tube. Pipe 3.2.1. linework alongside the runout edge. Pipe the top line with chocolate-coloured icing using a No 1 tube. Attach the candle to the cake top. Add some holly leaves, pine branches, a Christmas rose and a pine cone. Attach a red velvet ribbon to the cake board edge.

Painted side panels

78

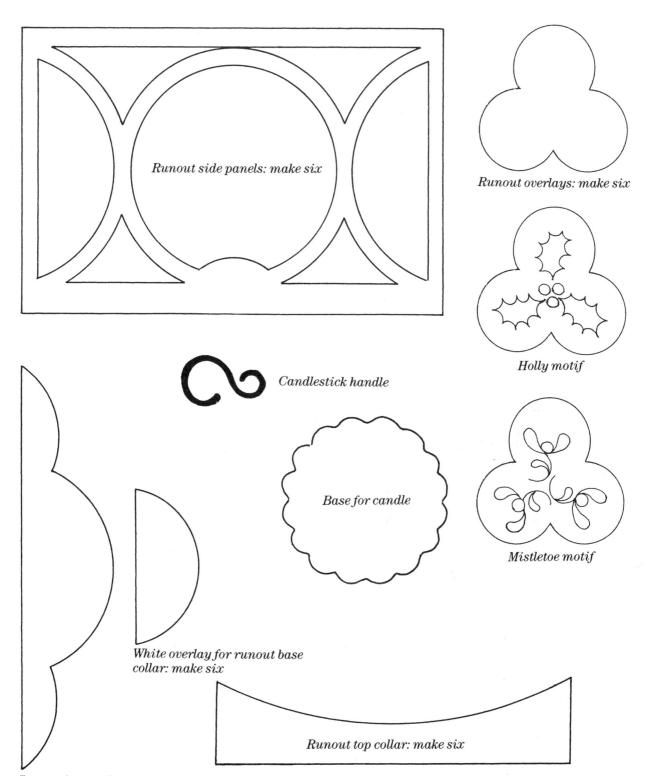

Runout side panels: make six

Runout overlays: make six

Holly motif

Candlestick handle

Base for candle

Mistletoe motif

White overlay for runout base
collar: make six

Runout top collar: make six

Runout base collar: make six

Making Royal Icing

Two recipes are given, one using fresh egg whites, the other using albumen-based powder which is available from specialist cake decorating shops. Both recipes can be made by hand or machine. The hand-mixing method will take longer than the easier machine method. When mixing icing in a machine use the slowest speed.

QUANTITIES

20cm (8in) round cake
600g (1¼lb) – royal icing
1¼ times recipe

20cm (8in) square cake
720g (1½lb) – royal icing
1½ times recipe

Ensure that the bowl and all other equipment to be used is free of grease. Wash everything in hot soapy water, followed by a hot water rinse. Allow the equipment to dry naturally or use a clean tea towel.

Royal icing using fresh egg whites

2½+ egg whites
450g (1lb/4 cups) icing (confectioner's) sugar (finely sieved)

Note: Depending upon the quantity of egg white in each egg, extra may be required

Break up the egg whites in a bowl using a fork, then lightly whisk until frothy. Add about a quarter of the sieved sugar and mix well using a wooden spatula. Add the remaining sugar gradually, lightly mixing after each addition. Stir round the sides of the bowl to incorporate any dry sugar. Continue lightly beating the mixture, either by hand or machine until firm peaks are formed when the spatula or machine beater is withdrawn. Under-mixed icing will be heavy, glossy and slightly creamy in colour.

Royal icing using albumen-based powder

12.5g (½oz/⅔ teaspoon) albumen-based powder
90ml (3floz/⅓ cup) water
450g (1lb/4 cups) icing (confectioner's) sugar (finely sieved)

Gently whisk the albumen powder into the water. The resulting mixture will be quite lumpy and will stick to the whisk. Do not try to whisk out the lumps at this stage, instead leave the mixture to stand for 15 minutes. Stir the mixture, and the lumps should dissolve.

Strain the solution into the bowl and add half of the sugar, mixing well with a wooden spatula. Add the remaining half of the sugar and continue mixing until all dry icing sugar is incorporated. Scrape down the sides of the bowl and lightly beat the mixture by hand or machine until the desired peak is reached.

Runout Icing

Use royal icing made up to normal piping consistency as described, which hasn't been stored for a long period of time. Stored icing becomes very heavy, moist and glossy and will produce dull, crumbly runout pieces. If the icing is heavy, very lightly re-beat it for a few seconds before use.

Place the required amount of icing in a bowl and thin it down with a small amount of water or albumen. Albumen will produce stronger runouts with a better surface sheen, than would be achieved using water. Add the extra liquid a drop at a time until you achieve the correct consistency. Stir the icing, do not beat while incorporating the liquid. Beating the mixture will produce air bubbles in the icing. To judge the amount of liquid required, withdraw the spoon and form a ribbon of icing across the bowl, slowly count to 10. The icing should just run back into itself (all ripples subsided) as you reach 10.

Cover with a damp cloth and use as soon as possible. Do not store runout icing for later use.

Spoon sufficient runout into your piping bag; do not overfill. A piping tube is not required for flood work, simply cut a hole at the point of the bag to the size of a No2 tube. Cutting the hole too large will make control of the icing more difficult. More importantly, air bubbles will appear on the surface of the dry runouts as greyish spots. A faint crackling noise of the tiny air bubbles bursting should be heard as the icing is forced through the piping bag.

It is important to dry runouts as quickly as possible near a source of gentle heat, in order to obtain a good surface sheen and firm shape.

Store the icing in an airtight container to prevent it from crusting over. Do not refrigerate.

Always clean down the inside of the storage container before replacing the lid.

For a softer icing, add 3.5ml (½ teaspoon) of glycerine for each 450g (1lb) of icing sugar used. Do not add glycerine to royal icing intended for run-out work.

For delicate tints and general colour work, use paste or liquid colours to colour the royal icing. For stronger colours such as Christmas red, chocolate-brown and black use special paste colours. These strong colours develop as the icing stands for about 30 minutes, so don't be tempted to add too much at the mixing stage.

PRINTED IN BELGIUM BY
proost
INTERNATIONAL BOOK PRODUCTION